PRAISE FOR *CHA̲[...]*
YOU DON'T WANT[...]

"Now here's a title that will challenge you to the core: *Chasing a God Don't Want to Catch*. Darren Wilson has an unusual gift to get readers to own up to thoughts and feelings they may never want to admit to or say out loud. He is raw, without being crass. He is vulnerable, without needing pity from his reader. His honesty helps us to admit to things previously ignored. His humor helps us to swallow the medicine of correct biblical perspective. And his insights bring hope where we've wandered about, needing authentic faith. I believe this book will help countless people find their 'true north' in understanding the heart of God and the purpose for their lives."

—BILL JOHNSON, SENIOR LEADER, BETHEL CHURCH,
REDDING, CALIFORNIA; AUTHOR OF *THE WAY*
OF LIFE AND *RAISING GIANT-KILLERS*

"Darren Wilson has an uncanny ability to communicate complex spiritual truths in such a tangible way. In this book, Darren shares candidly and humorously from his own life the issues he had with God, and in doing so, helps the reader get past their own. As you read this masterpiece, I encourage you to open up your heart. God is transforming the lives of a generation, who in turn will transform the culture around them. I believe God is going to use this book as a catalytic tool in His hands to awaken the hearts of multitudes around the globe."

—DARREN DAVIS, SENIOR PASTOR, THE HARBOUR
CHURCH, FORT LAUDERDALE, FLORIDA

"Darren Wilson's honesty and sense of humor is refreshing and there is no shortage of it in his new book *Chasing a God You Don't Want to Catch*. This is a book for all of us who have wrestled and doubted, questioned and ran. Darren's story reminds us that God meets us right where we are, even when it's messy!"

—KIM WALKER-SMITH, JESUS CULTURE

"Darren once again captures the essence of what it looks like to live with, follow, and relate to a God who is both a Father and a Judge. I have had the privilege of walking with Darren through some of his most painful and vulnerable life moments and have seen the revelations and the truths he communicates truly lived out by him. His emphasis on transformation as a developmental process that God takes us through is a real key to bringing glory to God. Darren takes the reader on a fun and encouraging encounter that ultimately leads to a greater revelation of who Jesus Christ is—'when you see Me, you see the Father.'"

—BRYAN SCHWARTZ, PASTOR, GLOBAL LEADERSHIP TEAM, CELEBRATION CHURCH, JACKSONVILLE, FLORIDA

"Darren Wilson is more than a communicator. His films and books have the simple and profound ability to communicate who God is in a deep and personal way. I have found my own freedom in what he has given to the world in his films, yet through this book I have found a more active dialogue with God. This is a must-read for anybody who has grappled with the very powerful concept of who God is, if He is, why He is, and the truth that He is actually for you!"

—CYNTHIA GARRETT, host of *THE SESSIONS* on TBN, AUTHOR, TV PERSONALITY, EXECUTIVE PRODUCER, FOUNDER OF CGM, WWW.CYNTHIAGARRETT.ORG

"Darren has put his pursuit of God on display for thousands to see through his movies and TV shows for years now, and having the privilege to participate in that journey myself, I can safely say that this book represents the *reason* for that journey. His dynamic writing style allows us a glimpse into the human experience as we attempt to wrestle with the mystery of God. This book will help both followers of Jesus and those still seeking to see their stories as a part of a much greater story. Darren gives beautiful, thoughtful language emphasized by biblical narrative to help us all explore the depths of God's love and power of hope, while not negating the great disconnect between what we say we want and how God actually gets us there."

—JAKE HAMILTON, WORSHIP LEADER AND SONGWRITER

"I listen deeply to a person whose goal above all else is to be a friend of God. Darren Wilson doesn't just talk the talk. I have seen Darren walk the authentic faith walk, not to have a big ministry or to put on a show for man, but for the pure joy of being a friend of God. If your heart has caught this same passion, you're going to want to read this book."

—JAMIE GALLOWAY, AUTHOR OF *SECRETS OF THE SEER*, JAMIEGALLOWAY.COM

"Darren has a history of finding himself in the overall narrative of God and His people. Darren simply wants to know God, and he is a phenomenal storyteller of the greatest story of all time. Darren has blessed us for years through his films and books. In this particular book, you will follow Darren's journey as he finds his own story through the narrative of Scripture, while he also wrestles through his own doubts, struggles, and questions. Darren writes as a friend of God, and no matter where you are on your journey, you will surely be blessed as you read this book.

—CHAD NORRIS, SENIOR PASTOR, BRIDGEWAY CHURCH, GREENVILLE, SOUTH CAROLINA

CHASING
A GOD
YOU
DON'T
WANT TO
CATCH

CHASING A GOD YOU DON'T WANT TO CATCH

DARREN WILSON

EMANATE
BOOKS

Published in Nashville, Tennessee, by Emanate Books, an imprint of Thomas Nelson. Emanate Books and Thomas Nelson are registered trademarks of HarperCollins Christian Publishing, Inc.

Thomas Nelson titles may be purchased in bulk for educational, business, fund-raising, or sales promotional use. For information, please e-mail SpecialMarkets@ThomasNelson.com.

Unless otherwise noted, Scripture quotations are taken from the ESV® Bible (The Holy Bible, English Standard Version®). Copyright © 2001 by Crossway, a publishing ministry of Good News Publishers. Used by permission. All rights reserved.

Scripture quotations marked NASB are from New American Standard Bible®. Copyright © 1960, 1962, 1963, 1968, 1971, 1972, 1973, 1975, 1977, 1995 by The Lockman Foundation. Used by permission. (www.Lockman.org)

Scripture quotations marked NIV are from the Holy Bible, New International Version®, NIV®. Copyright © 1973, 1978, 1984, 2011 by Biblica, Inc.® Used by permission of Zondervan. All rights reserved worldwide. www.Zondervan.com. The "NIV" and "New International Version" are trademarks registered in the United States Patent and Trademark Office by Biblica, Inc.®

Scripture quotations marked NKJV are from the New King James Version®. © 1982 by Thomas Nelson. Used by permission. All rights reserved.

Scripture quotations marked NRSV are from New Revised Standard Version Bible. Copyright © 1989 National Council of the Churches of Christ in the United States of America. Used by permission. All rights reserved.

All emphasis in Scripture belongs to the author.

ISBN 978-0-7852-3313-8 (eBook)
ISBN 978-0-7852-3310-7 (TP)

Library of Congress Control Number: 2020931448

Printed in the United States of America

20 21 22 23 24 LSC 10 9 8 7 6 5 4 3 2 1

DEDICATION

To my three children: Serenity, Stryder, and River. I have been through a lot in my life, but I have fought hard for the truth about the God I always talk to you three about. You must navigate this life yourselves. I'll help you when I can, but ultimately your lives are yours to live. My prayer is that the hard-fought victories of your old man will help you in some way embrace the Father's heart for you much sooner than I did. I pray the honesty and vulnerability of my wrestling match with God will help you in your own journeys. But more than anything, I hope this book shows you how truly wonderful the Father, Son, and Holy Spirit really are. And I pray that you will journey through this life with the desire to always walk in obedience to whatever the Father is asking of you each day.

I will fail you, as I have countless times in your lives. But He never will.

This book is for you.

Hopefully, you read it!

CONTENTS

FOREWORD

This is not just a good book, it's going to be a before and after moment for you if you read it. It is a book that is going to build your spiritual intelligence and help you to process through the maturing aspects of having a relationship with God. I am not one for comparisons, but it felt like reading C. S. Lewis with a sense of humor.

At the same time, this book is written by a normal guy who is brave enough to share his internal struggles with his relationship with God in a way that will cause you to find yourself square in the center of some of the pages of this book. Darren has the kind of cool where he is culturally relevant but isn't trying to ooze swag, which a lot of people who tackle the subject of a deeper life in God try to do. He is just walking with God in a way that is creating context and conversations for the rest of us.

That being said, as much as I love Darren, I was exhausted when he asked me to do this foreword. I won't do a foreword unless I read, agree with, and can promote the book. Let me be a little self-indulgent, but hopefully not self-important. When Darren asked me to do this, I looked down on my own writing to-do list. I saw my own two book deadlines, five forewords, and more than twenty endorsements publishers had requested, as well as multiple journalism articles that are half done. Darren is enough of a real friend that I had to consider it, but I was reluctant. Then I actually read the book. I will make a very honest statement: *I needed this book.* You probably do too—especially if you, or someone you know, hasn't quite worked out why you believe what you believe.

As I finished Darren's manuscript I headed to the airport. The book left me thinking deeply, pondering in my heart some of the principles that all of us who with deep faith wrestle with. Darren gave me new language, and I kept circling back to some of the points in the book. When he asks the question What will God take from me? or defines point by point a God who is Love according to 1 Corinthians 13, it was so much to take in and felt beautiful to my soul.

I jumped in my Uber and the driver and I got into quite a conversation. He was raised in a harsh religious expression of Christianity, and he knew just enough of who God is and what Christianity is to consider himself saved, because he has to be saved. But did he really want to be saved? Not based on his understanding of how it all worked. That is a terrible place to be, to know just enough to have to but not enough to want to. And that is where so many people find themselves. We had a beautiful conversation and Darren's book helped SO MUCH! I was able to basically counsel him and help move him forward in what I would consider a foundational way, simply because I had just read brilliant language and process from Darren for some of the things that were tripping the driver up. Talk about immediate gratification!

It made me think more deeply about a common struggle at

work in most Christians. Sometimes we know enough to agree with certain principles that may be confusing or grating to our current frame of mind or heart, but sometimes we agree only because we're supposed to, or out of fear of hell (see that chapter in this book). The Bible was meant to be a relational book that provides people who read it with the inner process and workings of God's heart and His love for us. Pursuing Him doesn't lead us into confusion, but helps us to live sanely in a world full of confusion.

This book reminded me of some my own wrestling with some of the deeper and larger questions I had about life and God. I remember a conversation I had with my father that reminds me of what this book will do for you. I had a good father. He wasn't the sharpest connector in the toolshed, but he fought hard for a heart-to-heart relationship. One time we were talking about my frustration with God. I told him I always felt like I was performing but that I was always failing. "God wants me to be holy? I fail that every day!" My relationship with God had been growing stunted because I had a wrong understanding in my identity of what He wanted, this time around the issue of holiness. My Christianity just felt like I had to be sinless, and I felt like I was failing all the time, which then brought on shame, performance, and fear.

My dad sat me down and said, "Son, I used to struggle with pornography before I was a Christian and it was a bad struggle. Part of what happened when I became a Christian is I started to value your mom more than I valued pornography or any other lust or potential woman. When I used something else that the Bible shows us not to, just to meet a need of lust, I would feel disconnected from your mom. The more I fell in love with her, I just couldn't bear to lose any ground with her. I quit pornography to protect our love. That's why you don't see me struggle with lust toward other women and why I don't have a secret habit of some sort. When you love someone so much you don't want to compromise or lose ANYTHING in that love, you will protect it at all cost. That's how we are supposed to practice relationship with God and that is what I would call walking in holiness."

It was an "aha" moment for me. A simple lesson that our Christianity and our holiness isn't a religious trophy but a race we run to protect love at all costs by saying no to anything that stops true love toward God or those He has put in our lives. After that I stopped performing for God and trying to be sinless. I started trying to build something so real with Him that I would want to fight to protect the quality of our relationship.

Darren's book reminded me of being mentored by my father and mother. It felt like someone was taking complicated questions and nurturing me so that I could come to new conclusions and begin to untangle some of the knots in my soul.

If this is your first experience with Darren, know this: he is an expert storyteller, but he also presents his sometimes messy and always vulnerable interior process in a social and cultural apologetic that is married to theology. I love that he brings up complicated issues and has no fear in sharing his own discouragement or even borderline disgust with some of the principles of Christianity. Not satisfied to just know the principle, Darren needed to experience who God is in His love, which is what he has done in his films. I have read other theologians, the postmodern guys, the apologetics forerunners, and just plain great Bible teachers who have tackled many of the same topics. But often they either get stuck halfway or offer no hope that a living relationship with God can change your whole perspective regardless of the internal battle you may be having.

It takes the Bible and God's heart at work within us to make sense of this amazing world He has placed us in, and Darren shows this as beautifully and as completely as someone can in one volume.

Through his movies, Darren has offered dozens of glimpses of the struggle of man and God's supernatural answers, but in this book, *Chasing a God You Don't Want to Catch*, we find the core belief system that Darren was trapped in, getting reformed by the very God who pursues us all. The way Darren shares these stories and this narrative—you are going to find yourself relating and wanting to experience God so you can come to the same kinds of conclusions. Like Darren says, God isn't a spicy meatball, but is gentle and . . . okay, okay, you're going to have to read about that in the end.

I know I mentioned it when I started this, but it bears repeating. In this book, Darren reminds me of a modern-day C. S. Lewis with a humorous streak. The creative thoughts, passion for Jesus, and hunger for healthy and livable theology that Darren writes from make me anxious for whatever else will come out of this normal man who has simply embraced an extraordinary God.

SHAWN BOLZ

TV and Podcast Host (*Exploring the Prophetic*, CPN; *Translating God*, TBN; *Exploring the Industry*, CBN NEWS)

Author and Journalist (*Translating God, Through the Eyes of Love, Breakthrough Prophecies, Prayers and Declarations*)

WWW.BOLZMINISTRIES.COM

INTRODUCTION

I think I always loved God. I just didn't like Him very much. And I certainly didn't trust Him at all.

Being a filmmaker, I am often asked to speak at churches or conferences, and I'm pretty sure I'm never quite what they were expecting. Most people see my movies and think I'm going to be a ball of profound faith and piercing wisdom. But what they get is a guy with a lot of scars and bruises from a lifetime of wrestling with God. What I've found, literally everywhere in the world, is that the vast majority of Christians have those exact same scars and bruises, but they never feel comfortable enough to talk about them.

I always used to say I wanted more of God. I'd sing the worship songs about yearning for more and desperately desiring God more than the air I breathe, but the truth was, deep down I knew what I was singing wasn't true. I didn't want more of God because to me He wasn't safe. I knew the closer I got to Him, the more challenging He would make my life. So I spent decades trying to do just enough Christian stuff to not feel like a total loser, yet also working hard to keep God at a safe enough distance that He wouldn't get dangerous.

The time has come for us to be honest with ourselves (and God) and just say it like it is. Faith is hard. And many of us, despite how much we try to disguise it on Sunday, simply aren't doing that great. We want God, but—you fill in the blank.

I want to speak to the doubters, the misfits, the posers who know they're posing, as well as those who think this is normal faith behavior. I want to talk to the Christians who know all the right answers but are living a life where those answers don't make a ton of sense anymore—the unseen majority, the ones who stay quiet because everyone else seems to have this faith thing figured out. I can assure you that you are not alone in your frustration.

The Bible is filled with characters who wouldn't be welcomed into most churches, but the ones who made a mark were the ones who reached out for God and wrestled with Him. Israel, God's chosen people, literally means "one who wrestles with God." He is not afraid of your questions, your doubts, or your anger. What He cannot engage with is your pretending. Your being fake. His ultimate desire is friendship with you—but true friendship is often a bit messy. It requires honesty and trust. You say you're chasing after God, but do you really want to catch Him? For most people, the answer is "probably not."

Let's try to change that, shall we?

/1/

THE BATTLEFIELD
OF THE MIND

*Do not conform to the pattern of this world, but be
transformed by the renewing of your mind. Then
you will be able to test and approve what God's will
is—his good, pleasing, and perfect will.*
—ROMANS 12:2 NIV

I have a vivid memory from years ago of sitting in church and
mentally checking out as soon as the sermon began. At the
time I was a college professor and I had yet to make my first film,
Finger of God. My faith had become as stale as dry bread. I never
struggled with belief in God or Jesus or atonement, but, after
years of participating in a Christianity that felt toothless, I had
sunk into a kind of malaise of predictable and despairing faith. I
continued to believe because deep down I knew it was right, but
my belief was stunted and thin—like a green bean that's been in
the sun too long.

I had "idea notebooks" that I took with me everywhere. Whenever an idea—big or small—would flit into my consciousness, I wrote it down. One day, as soon as the sermon started, I pulled out my notebook and began daydreaming. I'm sure the people around me thought I was taking notes on the sermon. Yeah, right.

On our drive home from church, my wife asked what I thought about the sermon and mentioned it seemed like something that would strike me as interesting. I admitted I hadn't listened to a word of it. This was the state of my faith for a very long time. More than once, I was accused of having a faith that was too locked in my mind, and I was often encouraged to let go of my "head faith" and let God get hold of my heart. I was surrounded by people who seemed to be truly passionate about God, and while I was happy for them, for me it just wasn't that simple. How was I supposed to turn off my brain? Did I even want a faith I couldn't enjoy intellectually? And anyway, I didn't think I could turn off my mind if I wanted to. It essentially wouldn't even be me who was doing the believing at that point.

But it wasn't just a disinterest in going deeper with God that was my problem; I also happened to be the most judgmental guy in the room. As soon as the speaker would make some statement I didn't deem biblical, I'd write off the entire sermon. I'd judge the song list for worship. I'd judge the lyrics. I'd judge the worship team's lack of professionalism. I'd judge the aesthetics of the church building. I'd judge the inadequate parking space. I'd judge that guy sitting in the third row who looked like he was judging everything. The list could go on forever. Between my spiritual malaise and my judgmental attitude, I had created a perfect storm of disinterest and pride. It was an exhausting spiritual existence, but what else could I do? Giving in to God and going after Him for real was out of the question. I mean, I wasn't *that* crazy.

I used to think my mind was the problem, that it was the thing keeping me from a vibrant, loving relationship with God. But that was a gross miscalculation on my part because, as we'll discover, the mind is the true battlefield of the heart. Faith isn't about turning off your mind to simply become a gullible lemming following orders. Faith is about turning your mind in the right direction. Once you come into agreement with not only who God is but what He desires, you'll begin to live the life of faith the way it was intended, and your faith will become less about just believing theological truths and more about making a conscious decision of trust. Trust, in the end, is the essence of faith.

As an observer of the world, perhaps the most difficult observation I have made is that Christianity doesn't seem to be doing much for people. If the ultimate goal is heaven, then sure, it's keeping a lot of people out of hell, but what about the life we're living right now? Surely Christ meant for us to experience much more than simply white knuckling it through life until we die, when the *real* fun will begin. When I read the Gospels, that's not the Jesus I see. I see a Jesus who was constantly meeting people in the realness of their lives and who brought freedom, healing, and a new state of mind to live from.

Look at the story of Zaccheus, for instance. "Zaccheus was a wee little man, and a wee little man was he," was a song I often sang as a child. His story seemed less about God's transformational power and more about a super-short dude who got lucky because he had the bright idea to climb a tree. But the story found in Luke 19 reveals something fascinating about human nature and the impact of truly encountering Jesus.

Jesus is rolling into Jericho with His crew when we are introduced to Zaccheus. We aren't told much about him, but we're told enough. He was the chief tax collector in the region and very rich. Tax collection back in the day wasn't like it is now, with strict rules and regulations and everything designed to make sure things are on the up and up. Jewish tax collectors worked for the Roman government, and they were notoriously dishonest. In Jewish culture, they couldn't serve as witnesses or judges and were expelled from the synagogue. And this guy wasn't just a tax collector; he was the guy who oversaw *all* the tax collectors in the region. So you can imagine the kind of reputation he had.

But for whatever reason, Zaccheus wants to get a glimpse of Jesus. He'd probably heard some of the crazy stories spreading across the region about this guy who was healing people and slaying demons, and my guess is Zaccheus was simply curious. But of course, when you're dealing with God, a tiny crack is all He needs to blow up your life.

There was a slight problem, though: Zaccheus was a wee little man. As the messianic parade is passing by, there are too many people in front of him, and obviously no one is going to help him get a better view. So he runs ahead and climbs a tree. Most people probably view this as proof of Zaccheus's hunger to see Jesus, but I can't help but notice how humiliating this probably was for him. Here's a rich guy everyone hates, he most likely already has a few emotional triggers around being so short, and now everyone sees him climbing a tree like a doofus.

I wonder if Jesus noticed Zaccheus because people were pointing and laughing at him. Regardless, Jesus stops in His tracks and calls Zaccheus by name (a baller prophetic move for sure), then invites Himself to Zaccheus's house. Luke 19:6 tells us that Zaccheus welcomes Jesus into his home gladly, so at least the host wasn't put off by the request. In fact, this is a perfect example of Jesus meeting someone in the throes of their sinful behavior.

All through the Gospels we see that the outcasts of society never ran from Jesus but instead ran to Him. I think His purity and love is most attractive to those who are considered the dirtiest, because they realize there is no way they can clean themselves up on their own. Religious people at least have some rituals and religious actions to make them feel like they are aiding things along in the redemption process. Religious people also have the most to lose (their personal status quo, the respect of other religious people, their religious reputations) by exposing their sin to Jesus. The outcasts have no pride to protect because they know most religious people don't like them anyway.

We have no idea what kind of dinner guest Jesus was, but we do see the outcome. Presumably through the sheer power of encountering the goodness and grace of Jesus, Zaccheus does something that very few people would do. He declares that he is going to give half of his money to the poor and pay back, four times over, anyone he has cheated. This is like repentance on steroids. And it all happened simply because Jesus invited Himself over for dinner.

I have a sneaking suspicion that Christians who consistently struggle or who show little sign of the fruits of the Spirit haven't encountered the real Jesus. They may have encountered the *idea* of Him and accepted that idea as true, but that is a far cry from encountering Him in person.

This was always my biggest frustration with God: my

complete inability to interact with Him on a physical level. I have heard it said that we are more spiritual beings than we are physical ones, and while that may be true, sometimes I just want a hug. I want to feel the ones I love, and not in the mystical, ethereal sense. I want an embrace. But with God I can never have that. He is the one I love most of all, but He remains frustratingly invisible and intangible.

What changed my trajectory from an angry, frustrated Christian to a more content, frustrated Christian was an encounter with this invisible God of the universe. I have talked at length about this encounter in my previous books, so I won't get into it here because the details aren't important. What is important is that my spirit man felt Him, and my spirit eyes saw Him. And what I encountered was a love unlike anything I'd ever experienced. And this love changed me. Just not in the way you might think.

I used to think that in order to change, all anyone needed was a powerful encounter with God. After all, wasn't it an encounter with Jesus that transformed Saul into Paul? Didn't we just see Zaccheus changed through encountering Jesus? Well, yes and no.

Paul and Zaccheus repented as a result of their encounters, which is obviously transformative in itself. But to repent is to turn away from something and head in a different direction, which is only the first step in our transformation. The problem many Christians have is they believe the encounter is the engine to transformation when it is merely the key to start the engine. So we chase one encounter after another, like drug addicts looking for our next Holy Spirit hit, desperately trying to get the ultimate high that will supposedly solve all our problems.

But remember, it was Paul himself who showed us the way

to transformation, and it doesn't involve getting knocked to the ground and being blinded for three days. We are not transformed by encounters, by worshiping more, or by fasting. We are transformed by the renewing of our minds. "Do not conform to the pattern of this world, but be transformed by the renewing of your mind" (Rom. 12:2 NIV).

How you think in many ways defines who you are. Many will say that what you do defines who you are, because talk is cheap, but how you think directly influences what you do—it's the root source of all your decisions. For instance, you might say you believe that stealing is wrong. But the question isn't whether you think it's wrong, but *how* wrong do you think it is? Is it wrong in all ways, case closed? Is it wrong unless you are stealing something for your or another's survival? Is it wrong inasmuch as it doesn't hurt the people you might be stealing from? Is it still wrong if you stole something accidentally and don't return it after you realize the truth of what you did? What about stealing something because you think the good that will come from it justifies the crime? People do this with my movies all the time. They rip them and put them up online and then get mad at us when we make them take them down because what they did is, you know, illegal. But they think my movies should be free, so it doesn't matter that they're breaking the law. It's righteous sin, I guess.

However you answer these questions, what you think about stealing in the circumstance you find yourself in will decide what you do in that circumstance. It's the constant battle of the flesh that Paul talked about: "For I do not do the good I want to do, but the evil I do not want to do—this I keep on doing" (Rom. 7:19 NIV).

Obviously there is a war being waged between our flesh and

our spirit man. Paul confirmed this when he said, "For in my inner being I delight in God's law; but I see another law at work in me, *waging war against the law of my mind* and making me a prisoner of the law of sin at work within me" (vv. 22–23 NIV). Many of us are prisoners to the sin in our lives because we have not won the war in our minds, and we haven't won the war in our minds because we have not been transformed by renewing them!

Christianity was never designed to be a safety net from hell. God's purpose all along has been to rescue His children from death (both spiritually and physically) and to return us to the way things were in the garden before sin entered the picture. In the garden God walked with Adam and spoke with him in the cool of the day—He enjoyed relationship and friendship with Adam. And ultimately, this is God's desire for all of us: that we would be restored to relationship and friendship with Him. It is this relationship and friendship that brings about true change in our lives, but it can only be had when we fully understand the nature and heart of God. And understanding is a thing of the mind.

Transformation must be the goal of our faith. I used to be a prisoner of my mind because I completely misunderstood who God was. This misunderstanding was the result of a mistaken view of various stories in the Bible that I thought showed an untrustworthy God (which we'll deal with more later in this book), and also by my own judgments against the Christians I was surrounded by. I didn't see much of a difference between them (or me) and non-Christians, except for what we believed about an invisible entity and a few differences in morality.

But since I didn't fully understand the nature of transformation and I didn't factor in the different journeys everyone was on, I allowed my judgments to cloud my reality. I didn't allow people to live in their own spiritual process because I didn't value spiritual process. I thought just because Scripture talked about Christian transformation that it was a given the moment you accepted Jesus as your Savior. And since very few people were living out this transformation, it meant that they must all be hypocrites and, well, that I must be a hypocrite too. Enter shame and guilt for my own hypocrisy, and you've got a great recipe for a very unhappy Christian experience.

But there is good news. Transformation is possible. Changing destructive and sinful behavior is possible. Loving those who hurt you, forgiving the unforgivable, is possible. The secret is found in changing the way you think.

I would be remiss if I didn't finish the verse we've been looking at, because leaving it unfinished would be to turn this into a self-help remedy, and that's definitely not what we're after. I want true, gut-level change in how I operate my life and interact with others. I don't just want to engage in "mind over matter." That's not sustainable, and it's not true transformation.

Romans 12:2 starts off by telling us that we are to be transformed by the renewing of our minds, but it is to a very specific purpose: "then you will be able to test and approve what God's will is" (NIV). Why in the world is this the goal? How does "testing and approving what God's will is" lead us into a deeper friendship with Him?

The answer is found in understanding the core value of friendship with God.

/2/

TRUSTING A
DANGEROUS GOD

I f it's true that how you think defines who you are, then what you think about God is the most important question of your life. All life on earth was created by God and for God, and for the most part everyone is wrestling with what they think about God. For some He's a tyrant, and they reject Him as unworthy of their love. For others He's a genie, and when He doesn't give them what they want, they either pout or lose their secure footing. Some view God as a kind of force that can be found in everything—not a personal being, mind you, but more like a providential mist that isn't super interested in rules or details but only in the big picture of things. Some view God as a puppet master, causing all the good and all the bad in the world. They are elated when good things happen but devastated when tragedy strikes. Others view Him as a figment of people's imaginations. What you think about God is who God is to you, and it affects every aspect of your life. It's your spiritual reality, even if it may be entirely wrong.

Hebrews 11:6 tells us that without faith it is *impossible* to please God. This verse fascinates me because it is so direct. I think a lot of people miss this and they replace *faith* with *religious activity*. We often think that the more we do for God, the better we are with Him. If I can just do my devotions on a more regular basis, or if I can just soak in His presence more, or if I can serve more at my church, then I know that will please Him. Well, I'm sure He will find anything you do for Him pleasing, but don't forget the one thing you must have if that is your goal. You have to have faith. But what exactly *is* faith?

The definition is pretty straightforward. Merriam-Webster says faith is "complete trust." So then, how much trust must we have in God for it to qualify as faith? Jesus said if we have faith the size of a mustard seed we can see great things. So I guess even the tiniest amount of trust in God counts for something. But I would like to make the argument that if our goal in life is to please God, then the main thing we should be focusing on is our faith level. If it's impossible to please God without trusting Him, then wouldn't it make sense that the more we learn to trust Him, the more pleasing we are to Him?

Why does it need to be this way? Why is God so preoccupied with our faith in Him? Why is it such a big deal?

When Saul screws up big time and basically loses his kingship (1 Sam. 15), he doesn't lose everything because he kills someone or commits adultery (shoot, David did both those things). He loses it all because he has no faith in God and this lack of faith leads to disobedience. The Lord told Saul to go bust up a town named Amalek, and he was to spare no one—not even the animals—in this mission. This was divine retribution for stuff Amalek had done to Israel, so Saul heads out on a military sortie. He does what he's told—mostly. Saul takes the king of Amalek, Agag, hostage, and keeps a bunch of the best animals to offer as a sacrifice to God. It seems like Saul has good intentions, but unfortunately it's not what God asked him to do.

The prophet Samuel rolls in, and Saul is feeling pretty good about himself. He has even built a little monument to himself to mark the occasion, like an idiot. Saul proudly tells Samuel that he's done what God asked him to do. Then Samuel drops the hammer: "What then is this bleating of the sheep in my ears, and the lowing of the oxen which I hear?" (1 Sam. 15:14 NKJV). Saul tries to put a nice spin on it, but Samuel wants none of it.

> "Has the LORD as great delight in burnt offerings and
>   sacrifices,
> as in obeying the voice of the LORD?
> Behold, *to obey is better than sacrifice,*
> *and to heed than the fat of rams.*
> For rebellion is as the sin of witchcraft,
> and stubbornness is as iniquity and idolatry.
> Because you have rejected the word of the LORD,
> he has also rejected you from being king." (1 Sam.
>   15:22–23 NKJV)

Dang. Saul is toast. And all because he didn't obey the voice of the Lord. He didn't trust God's word. He didn't have faith but did what seemed right in his own eyes. Lesson #1: *If you want God, you've got to take Him on His terms.*

We know faith is a big deal to God, if not *the* biggest, but again I ask, why? While I realize there are three currencies in God's kingdom (faith, hope, and love) and 1 Corinthians 13 tells us plainly that the greatest of these is love, we still can't avoid the utter importance of faith as explained in Hebrews 11:6, particularly when it comes to pleasing God. I would argue that while it's impossible to please God without faith, if your faith isn't grounded in love, the whole thing kind of falls apart. Hope then is the glue that holds them all together. But for our purposes, I want to focus on this slippery little thing called faith, since the battleground we're dealing with is the mind, and faith is very much a mind thing.

A frustration that has never left me is the fact that God is invisible. When He asked me to make films about Him, my first thought was, *Uh, God, You do realize that film is a visual medium and You're, well, not.* Figuring out new ways to make an invisible God visible is the biggest hurdle I have in making my movies. It's like trying to film air. The only way you can even tell it's there is when the wind blows. So I have to try to find situations where God's wind is blowing on people.

In my book *Finding God in the Bible*, I talk at length about "God's invisibility cloak." Maybe it's because I'm a filmmaker that I obsess about God's invisibility so much, but I think it's a thing for a lot of other people too. I mean, let's face it, if you're a Christian, you literally believe in an invisible man. As in, an invisible man is your best friend. No wonder the world thinks we're nuts sometimes.

When I examined the invisibility problem, I found a possible explanation. There are two wildly different instances of God "showing" Himself to people in Scripture, and both can teach us a lot about God's nature.

The first is found in Exodus 33. Moses has gone up Mount Sinai and is hanging out with God. The two friends are talking about Israel, with Moses reminding the Lord that these are His people after all, so, you know, don't smite them, please. Yes, they're a dysfunctional tribe, but they're His dysfunctional tribe. God shows great affection for Moses, saying, "You have found favor in my sight, and I know you by name" (Ex. 33:17 NRSV). So Moses realizes he's holding the golden ticket, and he just goes for broke and asks to see God's full glory. What a request! Shockingly, God decides to grant his request, but with the caveat that Moses only be able to look upon His back. If he looked at God's face, he'd die. Like, *Raiders of the Lost Ark* face-melting die. So God puts Moses in a cave and passes by, allowing Moses to see His full goodness. Man, I'm not jealous of much, but this one is off-the-charts cool.

After this little love fest, God makes new tablets for Moses to take to the people with His commandments, and Moses scurries down the mountain. But he doesn't realize that because he just literally saw God, his face is now glowing. Everyone freaks out when they see Moses, and he has to wear a veil because the people simply cannot deal. Understand what's going on here— the people are freaking out at the aftereffect of someone else seeing God. Just imagine what would have happened if they'd seen Him with their own eyes!

There will come a point in time when the entire world *will* see Him in His fullness with their own eyes. God minced no words when He said:

> "By myself I have sworn,
>   my mouth has uttered in all integrity
>   a word that will not be revoked:

> Before me every knee will bow;
>> by me every tongue will swear.
> They will say of me, 'In the LORD alone
>> are deliverance and strength.'
> All who have raged against him
>> will come to him and be put to shame."

(ISA. 45:23–24 NIV)

God is not messing around here, and He wants you to realize it. He swears by Himself (there is nothing higher) that what He's about to say will happen. And why is He so sure that this is going to happen, especially considering how horribly messed up the world is these days? Are we Christians suddenly going to become incredible witnesses for Him? That's highly doubtful. No, I think there's only one way for this event to happen, and it's going to come at the grand finale of life as we know it on earth. Whenever that "date and time that only the Father knows" comes, that will be the moment when God throws off His invisibility cloak and the whole world will see Him for who He truly is. At that moment, when He shows Himself clearly in all His goodness and glory, *every* knee will bow and every tongue will confess that He is indeed Lord of all.

But there's a funny little thing about love that most people forget. Love must be a choice. Its very nature demands freedom, and all love comes with the risk of rejection. It's why God gave man free will. You cannot have true love without the possibility of rejection. It's that possibility of rejection that all of us have faced at one time or another.

I have vivid memories of hiding in my parents' bathroom at age fifteen, staring at the beige phone I'd pulled in with me, trying to will myself to call a girl and ask her to go to the skating rink with me. But calling meant I'd have to admit I liked her and, good Lord, what if she said she didn't like me back? I'd sit and stare at that phone, but the fear of rejection was simply too great. I couldn't do it.

Yet God does it over and over and over again. He puts Himself out there, asking us to choose Him, to love Him like He loves us. And when we reject Him and His kindness for our own selfish desires, He simply looks for another opportunity to prove His love and grace once again. For many, it will be a lifetime pursuit, and they will never choose Him, usually because they never fully understand how wonderful He is. They look at His other kids and think their dysfunction is somehow His dysfunction. But we are all in need of a Savior, even when we've chosen Him. The war rages on around us, and it won't ever stop.

You see, God cannot reveal Himself to us physically, because if He were to do that our choice to love Him would cease to be a choice at all. Every knee would bow because no matter what you do or don't believe, if you were to see Him for who He is, not through the filters of our brokenness, but truly as He is—He'd be utterly irresistible. When that day comes, for those who have chosen to love Him when it was most difficult, our love will be made complete. For those who haven't, it will be a day filled with the greatest regret of their lives.

When Jesus showed Himself to His disciple Thomas after Thomas said he wouldn't believe that Jesus had been resurrected unless he saw it with his own two eyes, Jesus simply reiterated the importance of faith that God had instituted since Adam and Eve fell: "Blessed are those who have not seen and yet have believed" (John 20:29 NIV).

There is another curious Bible story where God reveals Himself to a man, but this experience is vastly different from the Moses moment. In 1 Kings 19, God has an encounter with the prophet Elijah.

First, a little context. Not too long before this encounter, Elijah had his ultimate boss moment on Mount Carmel when he went toe to toe with the prophets of Baal. Basically he challenged the demon worshipers to a duel to see whose God was greater. Elijah was a gentleman and let the priests of Baal go first, and they spent the next few hours asking their "gods" to light a pyre of wood on fire, with no success. They even resorted to cutting themselves, because apparently that was a thing. At one point Elijah got cheeky and asked them if maybe Baal stepped out for a bathroom break. When they finally gave up, Elijah went into full showstopper mode. He made them dig a hole around the pyre, then doused everything with so much water that it basically became an altar water park. Then he prayed and asked God to light the pyre. It ignited with so much fire that even the water in the hole dried up!

One would think that with that moment on your faith résumé, you wouldn't freak out when a lady named Jezebel says she's going to murder you. But apparently this Jezebel lady was rotten to the core and had been killing off the prophets of Israel with ruthless intensity. So Elijah splits and flees to a mountain because, you know, obviously God can't protect him from this lunatic. Oh how quickly we forget our own victories with God.

While Elijah is hiding out in a cave, the Lord finally comes to him. And this is where things get interesting. The Lord asks him, "What are you doing here, Elijah?" It's a curious question, but one laced with subtext. Obviously the Lord knows why Elijah is there. God is implying that Elijah's faith is leaving something to be desired at the moment. Elijah's reply reveals he just doesn't understand why the Lord is letting all this happen to him.

"I have been very zealous for the LORD, the God of hosts; for the Israelites have forsaken your covenant, thrown down your altars, and killed your prophets with the sword. I alone am left, and they are seeking my life, to take it away" (1 Kings 19:10 NRSV).

It's basically an "after all I've done for you" moment. You can almost hear the accusation in Elijah's voice. God's response is firm, swift, but also loving. "Go out and stand on the mountain before the LORD, for the LORD is about to pass by" (1 Kings 19:11 NRSV). Again reading the subtext, God isn't about to engage in a verbal back and forth with Elijah—He's just going to show him what's what. *You don't think you can trust Me? You don't think I can save you from your enemy? Well stand back, bub, because you're about to get a good dose of Me.* Based on what God did with Moses, we assume God is going to do His standard "God is about to reveal Himself" stuff and Elijah's going to start glowing too. Until the twist ending, of course . . .

> Now there was a great wind, so strong that it was splitting mountains and breaking rocks in pieces before the LORD, but the LORD was not in the wind; and after the wind an earthquake, but the LORD was not in the earthquake; and after the earthquake a fire, but the LORD was not in the fire; and after the fire a sound of sheer silence. When Elijah heard it, he wrapped his face in his mantle and went out and stood at the entrance of the cave. Then there came a voice to him that said, "What are you doing here, Elijah?" (1 Kings 19:11–13 NRSV)

Elijah is all of us in that moment. Something is happening in our lives and we are crying out to God. *Help me. Save me. Do something. Where are you?* And we are waiting for Him to send a wind of change that will break mountains and split rocks. We want an earthquake of action, to see our troubles experience upheaval as our He-Man smashes our enemies to powder. We want Him to send a fire to burn up our problems and surround us so we'll be safe. But God isn't in any of those things. We want it, and Elijah wanted it, because it is tangible. It is something we can see. But God is very clear with Elijah. He is not found in the tangible. Love is His endgame, and if we have to be frustrated at times because His invisibility isn't giving us exactly what we want and how we want it, then we're just going to have to deal with it. Because it's that invisibility that keeps love in play.

Silence. That's where God is found on that mountain. That is where He resides in our storms of life. He is not silent because He's unkind. He's silent because . . . well . . . we'll get to that in a later chapter.

When Elijah hears sheer silence, he knows God is there, and he wraps his face in his mantle because he knows he is about to experience God, and no eyes can look upon His face and live. He moves to the entrance of the cave, and God finally speaks again. "What are you doing here, Elijah?" God is so kind in how He deals with His weak kids. Elijah is one of His greatest prophets, yet here he is hiding out in a cave, fear gripping him, his faith in God next to nothing. Yet instead of lecturing him or punishing him or shaming him, God simply asks the same question He started with. The subtext the first time was, "What are you doing?" The subtext the second time is, "Do you see Me now? Do you trust Me?"

It is a tactic God will use again a few thousand years later, when the resurrected Jesus meets with Peter. The last time they had seen each other, Jesus turned to look at Peter just as Peter denied Him for the third time. The shame and guilt Peter must have felt as he ran off and "wept bitterly"! Yet when Jesus encounters His friend again, He asks three times if Peter loves Him. Jesus is so full of grace and mercy that He doesn't hold Peter's mistakes against him.

I think it may be God's invisibility that pushes faith to the top of the kingdom depth charts. God knows how difficult it is for us to believe in someone we can't see. "Blessed are those who haven't seen, yet still believe." He knows how quickly the reality of His presence fades from memory as the world of our senses returns to dominate our perception. It is precisely because faith is so difficult that God places such a high value on it.

Matthew 28:16–17 should put everyone at ease, because it reveals a core flaw inside all of us. Jesus has just risen from the dead, and the eleven disciples follow an angel's instructions to head back to Galilee and go to a mountain to wait for Jesus.

"When they saw him, they worshiped him; but some doubted" (Matt. 28:17 NRSV). Are you kidding me? The resurrected Jesus is standing in front of his closest friends, and even then, doubt creeps in. *Is this really Jesus? Am I really seeing what I think I'm seeing?* And even more interesting, Jesus doesn't address it at all. He simply describes the authority He now has and gives them their marching orders. He ends it in a beautiful way: "And surely I am with you always, to the very end of the age" (Matt. 28:20 NIV).

You're going to have to deal with your own doubts as you journey through this faith walk, but don't worry, Jesus isn't going anywhere. He'll walk with you always. Your doubts don't frighten or threaten Him one bit.

My life verses have become John 15:14–15. Jesus is talking to His disciples—us, really—and their (our) training time is over. It's go time. And this is what Jesus tells us: "You are my friends if you do what I command. I no longer call you servants, because a servant does not know his master's business. Instead, I have called you friends" (NIV). This is the ultimate goal for all Christians: to become friends with God. He's not looking for people to simply do His bidding like servants; He's looking for people who can walk with Him in the cool of the day and be at peace with Him. But the key to friendship with God, as Jesus makes quite clear, is obedience. And in order to be obedient, you must trust the person you're obeying. And what is trust? It is faith.

It is possible to love someone and not trust them. We all have people in our lives whom we love dearly, but man, we don't trust them to come through often. But think about your best friend in the world. I guarantee that person is someone you would trust with your very life. I would never share my deepest secrets with some people I love, but my best friend, he knows everything. The same is true for friendship with God. If I want to have a deep friendship with Him, I'm going to have to trust Him. And He's going to need to trust me too. What are you doing in your life that is fostering not just your trust in God, but His trust in you?

As I've spoken all over the world and shown my movies in hundreds of churches, it has become abundantly clear that I'm not alone. The church does not have a *loving* God problem, we have a *trusting* God problem. And it's an epidemic.

/3/

THE SIN GAME OF
HIDE AND SEEK

My own sin and the feelings of shame, guilt, and embarrassment that come with it have held me back from a deep, constant friendship with God for most of my life. And I'm pretty sure I'm not alone. It's a tale as old as humanity, and it is the Devil's greatest trick.

Let's see if this sounds familiar. You act like an idiot. Pick your poison: You were consumed with lust once again, you drank too much, you let your temper explode as you yelled at your kids, you treated someone like a piece of garbage, you gave in to your baser instincts and gossiped with your neighbor like an old lady at a knitting club. Whatever it is, you screwed up and you know it. You're now in the "afterhaze" of sin—that wasteland of guilt, shame, and self-loathing that forcefully reminds you that you are nowhere near a perfect creation in Christ. Far from it. You sometimes wonder if you're even a Christian at all.

What you do now is crucial. You've got two paths in front of you. One leads you straight to the cross, but you're going to have to get naked to go there. The other leads you farther into the wasteland, but at least you get to keep your clothes on. Once again, the battle line has been drawn, and it's all happening in your head. If your mind isn't renewed to a place of transformation, then you're going to lose this battle again and again.

Here is the mindset I've become familiar with in the sin afterhaze. Depending on my current spiritual state, it's usually one of the following:

- God is super ticked at me right now and is boiling with anger.
- I just hurt or inflicted pain on God somehow, and the Holy Spirit is grieving because of me. Shame on me.
- God has turned away from me because His holiness couldn't look upon my sinfulness. He'll come back when He cools off.
- Punishment is looming. Prepare for the worst.
- I may have just reached the threshold of God's patience with me. This was simply one time too many.

There are probably many more, but I think you get the idea. Whichever mindset I activate always leads to the same conclusion: I am in no way fit to approach God, and either He needs a time-out from me for a while, or I am going to have to do whatever I can to clean myself up before approaching Him again.

Is this really who God is and what He is like?

THE CYCLE BEGINS

The Bible tells of countless acts of sin, but it would probably do us good to go back to the beginning and look at how this horrible cycle began. Looking closely at the story of Adam and Eve also gives us a pretty interesting glimpse of God's nature and His response to our idiot decisions.

You probably know the story. God goes bananas creating the entire universe, earth included (he even created bananas!), and for His crown jewel He creates man and names him Adam. Adam loves his new digs, but there's something missing—he needs a lady friend. So God creates Eve from Adam's rib, and they only have eyes for each other (well, I guess jungle club was a bit empty—beggars can't be choosers). Anyway, God tells them they pretty much have the run of the place, with one tiny caveat. Apparently there's a tree nearby they're not allowed to eat from. But hey, there's every other kind of fruit and vegetable you can think of, so no worries, right? (My first question would have been, "Yeah, but where's the meat tree?")

One can assume that Adam and Eve enjoy some time of pure bliss and joy in their new outdoor crib. Genesis 3:8 gives us a tantalizing glimpse of what could have been for all of us, and it also reveals God's intended design for us and His creation. It simply reads, "Then the man and his wife heard the sound of the Lord God as he was walking in the garden in the cool of the day" (NIV). Goodness. God Himself hung out with Adam and Eve. They probably had dinners together. (I bet God's pasta bolognese was just divine.) The most loving being in the universe was their friend. That was always God's plan. But then the Devil shows up and makes them question God's goodness.

Not much has changed. As a child, I used to think that the fruit on the forbidden tree was magic or something. Like the apple in *Snow White*, it was full of poison or had some weird curse on it. But now I think it was probably just normal fruit—not much different than any of the other fruit in the garden. The only real difference was God asked them to simply obey, and He gave them a choice, because all love requires freedom of choice. And the Devil twisted His intentions into a lie laced with half-truth that sounded just plausible enough.

> And he said to the woman, "Has God indeed said, 'You shall not eat of every tree of the garden'?" And the woman said to the serpent, "We may eat the fruit of the trees of the garden; but of the fruit of the tree which is in the midst of the garden, God has said, 'You shall not eat it, nor shall you touch it, lest you die.'"
>
> Then the serpent said to the woman, "You will not surely die. For God knows that in the day you eat of it your eyes will be opened, and you will be like God, knowing good and evil."
>
> So when the woman saw that the tree was good for food, that it was pleasant to the eyes, and a tree desirable to make one wise, she took of its fruit and ate. (Gen. 3:1–6 NKJV)

The Devil is a liar, and his tactics haven't changed much. "Did God really say?" has been his go-to move since the beginning. He wants you to question God's goodness, His word, His promises. Because if he can get you started down a path of doubt, he can lead you onto the ultimate path of unbelief.

I find it interesting how the Devil shows his hand in this story. You can learn most of what you need to know about Satan's tactics right here. First, he'll jab you with doubt. Then, once he's got you confused, he'll hit you with his roundhouse: lies that have the dusting of truth. He's even done it with major world religions. Islam will tell you that, sure, Jesus is real, and He's even a great prophet. *But* He's not the Son of God. Mormonism sure sounds a lot like Christianity, but they have added to the Bible (actually creating new scriptures) and changed Jesus' nature to that of a created being. Jehovah's Witnesses adhere to the Bible, but they've changed bits of Scripture to bend to their belief system. There is the dusting of truth, but it's twisted in such a way that it is no longer pure and holy and true.

So with Eve, after questioning what she's heard, Satan hits her with: "You won't die" (a bald-faced lie), "for God knows that in the day you eat of it your eyes will be opened" (true), "and you will be like God, knowing good and evil" (true—but he conveniently leaves out the consequences). God only told them that if they ate of it, they would die. He didn't explain the intricacies of sin, because at that point they didn't know sin—they were perfect—so they would have had no way to understand what He was talking about. He simply asked them to be obedient.

But sin is disobeying God. Adam and Eve couldn't know what sin was—what good and evil was—until they had walked in disobedience. God wanted them to avoid that fate because knowledge of good and evil isn't something we need in order to be fulfilled. To abide in God's goodness is the bread of life that sustains us—and it is truly all we need.

But Eve took the bait, even thinking she was making a good decision. "So when the woman saw that the tree was good for food, that it was pleasant to the eyes, *and a tree desirable to make one wise*, she took of its fruit and ate" (Gen. 3:6 NKJV).

The Devil both lied to her and told her the truth. Yes, eating of the fruit would make her wise, but it would be a wisdom laced with death.

Eve eats, then she gives some to Adam. I often wonder what would have happened if Adam had refused. Would Eve have been banished, and would God then have given him another woman to be his companion? Would they have continued to coexist together, with some alternative spiritual reality kicking in where sinful and sinless live together somehow? We'll never know, because Adam proves to be just as dumb as Eve, and he doesn't even need the sly push from the Devil. And once they have both eaten, once they have both disobeyed God, the purity of God's creation is destroyed. They just screwed everything up for billions of people.

It would be good to pause here and think, because this is the key to understanding God's heart when it comes to friendship and how He views and reacts to His kids. You would expect the following scene: Adam bites the apple and suddenly the sky rips open, thunder booms, and the wrath and anger of God pour down in a pillar of fire. I mean, this is it. This is *the* moment that tears humanity from the presence of God. With this one decision, they have just made a way for all the horrors of evil. Murder. Rape. Child abuse. Pornography. Sex trafficking. The Holocaust. Genocide. Brutal dictatorships. Slavery. Racism. The list is literally endless. These two numbskulls couldn't say no to a simple temptation of fruit, and now the whole world is about to be plunged into the worst evil has to offer. And to top it all off, they just gave God's beloved Son a death sentence.

You would expect God to scream. You would expect Him to roar at them in anger. You would understand His raining down fire and vengeance on them. But remember, these two were His friends.

How, then, did God react when His friends committed a sin that would have infinitely more consequences than *anything* you've ever done, no matter how horrible? The answer should be enough to make all of us seriously question our spiritual hide-and-seek cycle.

> And they heard the sound of the LORD God walking in the garden in the cool of the day, and Adam and his wife hid themselves from the presence of the LORD God among the trees of the garden.
>
> Then the LORD God called to Adam and said to him, "Where are you?" (Gen. 3:8–9 NKJV)

God doesn't blow a gasket. He doesn't leave them until He can cool off. He *pursues* them. He knows what they've done, and His first instinct is to immediately move toward them.

Jesus gave us a similar glimpse of the Father's heart toward our sin when He told the parable of the prodigal son. A punk kid wants to strike out on his own, so he asks his old man for his inheritance early. The kid takes it and squanders it all—on a life of sin, no less—until he is broke and broken. He ultimately limps back toward his father's house, so desperate that he's willing to become a servant in his own home. But the father sees him at a distance and without hesitating runs to his boy.

This story Jesus told is astounding in more ways than one. It's more than a father being happy to see his son after he left home for a while. Middle Eastern culture, especially in the first century, would have raised an eyebrow at this seemingly feel-good story.

For one thing, a Middle Eastern man *never* ran. Remember, they weren't rocking Wranglers back then; they wore tunics, which meant that if a man wanted to run, he'd have to hike up his tunic so he wouldn't trip. In that culture it was humiliating and shameful to show your bare legs, but in this story, the father (representing our heavenly Father) couldn't care less. That's his son off in the distance, and his love for him inspires him to spurn his own vanity or cultural or religious standing.

But there's one more piece to this parable that's even more incredible. If a Jewish son in that culture lost his inheritance and then returned home, he'd have to undergo a community ceremony called the *kezazah*, literally a "cutting off." Basically, they would break a large pot in front of him, then flatly state, "You are now cut off from your people," and the entire community would reject him. He'd be an outcast. A pariah, forced to endure his shame and guilt forever. Sounds cheerful.

So it is quite possible, as Jesus told this story, that the listeners realized what was happening. This father wasn't just running because he was excited to see his son return home, he was actually running to catch his son before he reached the village. The father subjected himself to shame in order to keep his son from experiencing shame, to accept him before the community rejects him.

There would be no *kezazah* ceremony this time, because the father was bypassing with grace and forgiveness what should have happened to the son. And to top it all off, the father threw a massive party for his boy, and the entire village was invited. You can imagine the son was probably a little embarrassed by all the attention and more than a little confused by his father's reaction, but beyond all else, he was thankful for his father's love and he would never question it again. The only one who was truly upset by all this, at least as the story is told, was the older brother. The religious one. Because grace just doesn't seem fair to the religious mind.

And that's ultimately our problem, isn't it? As much as we want to look at the Pharisees and Sadducees and the leading religious leaders of Jesus' day as the bad guys, they were most of us dressed up in different clothing and bearing different titles. Most Christians are deeply rooted in a religious mindset, and because we *try* to be good and we don't commit *that* sin, it doesn't feel great when God's grace comes face-to-face with *them*. But even more than that, we have a really hard time accepting that same grace and love for ourselves when we have fallen short, because so much of our religious mindset is wrapped up in what we do for God and not *who we are in Christ*. We constantly slip out of a grace mindset and back into the worldly karma mentality. *You're going to get what you deserve.* But grace upends karma and makes it impotent.

And now, at the moment Adam and Eve have destroyed everything God has intended, He chooses to pursue them. "Where are you?" He asks. Think about that the next time you are in sin's afterhaze. God's reaction to you choosing disobedience and evil is never to hide from you. It's actually the opposite. We are the ones who run and hide. "Adam and his wife hid themselves from the presence of the LORD." Their shame made them fear a God of love. They knew what they had done. Their eyes were opened, all right. And they knew that punishment was coming.

But punishment didn't come. Consequences did, for sure, but not punishment. In fact, God not only pursues them, but when they admit that they are now ashamed of their nakedness, He takes things even further: "Also for Adam and his wife the LORD God made tunics of skin, and clothed them" (Gen. 3:21 NKJV).

God kills His own creation to cover their shame. God should be furious, but instead He comes to their aid. He goes against His own desires for His creation to not experience death just to bring peace to the sinners. And God's killing His creation to cover them is simply a foretaste of what He will ultimately have to sacrifice for the rest of us: His beloved Son.

And are you ready for the real kicker? Most people don't know this, because the art depicting it for centuries could never show the fullness of the crucifixion, but it was common practice for Romans to crucify people naked. It is highly likely that Jesus was not just brutally tortured and killed, but he was also exposed and humiliated as He hung on the cross completely naked. Sin makes us want to hide our nakedness from God, and Jesus' naked sacrifice restored the original intent—we can now approach God by shedding our sinful garments and being clothed in Jesus' righteousness.

THE ALL-TIMER

Let's talk about David, shall we? This dude was something else. He received the ultimate moniker, "a man after God's own heart," yet he committed one of the worst acts in the entire Bible. It's hard to understand sometimes why God picks certain people to be His friends. Obviously He sees something in their heart of hearts that He can work with, but man, some of them are a piece of work.

We can't really talk about David without first mentioning

Saul, who is the poster boy of what not to do when God selects you for greatness. The short version goes like this: Israel wants a king because apparently all the cool kids have one, so they cry out to the Lord to send one. God wants them to trust in Him alone, but He acquiesces to their desires (He loves us even when we're petulant and stupid) and anoints Saul king. Saul looks the part, and the prophet Samuel even says God would have had his line reign forever (1 Sam. 13:13). But Saul heads out to battle one day and disobeys God's command because he either doesn't trust God's timing or he views God as a religious checklist that leads him to victory (note, there is no relationship in either of these scenarios). God is not happy about this, and since He knows Saul's heart is never going to change, He tells him to take a hike. God's got His eyes set on someone else, someone who has the seeds of radical obedience inside him.

But then God decides to give Saul another chance, the very one we read about in the last chapter, with the Amalekites and the bleating sheep. Saul takes that information and *mostly* does what God asks of him, but he allows the king, Agag, as well as the best sheep and oxen, to live. And that's when God has seen enough. "Has the LORD as great delight in burnt offerings and sacrifices, as in obeying the voice of the LORD?" (1 Sam. 15:22 NKJV).

God desires obedience above all else. Now, I'll admit that this was one of the things that bugged me about God for most of my life, and I'll deal with this whole idea of God simply wanting us to shut up and be obedient in a later chapter. For now, let's just accept the fact that Saul was rejected as king because he didn't value the same things God valued.

But apparently David did.

So let's turn our attention back to the redhead with beautiful eyes (yup, David was probably a ginger). If you've had even an ounce of Sunday school in your past, you can probably fast-forward to where we need to go. David kills Goliath, is hunted by Saul for years, and eventually becomes king. There, we're caught up. Now let's get to David's extreme low point.

One night while the troops are off at war, David takes a nighttime stroll on his rooftop and sees a beautiful woman named Bathsheba bathing. I used to be a little confused by this story. Then I visited Israel and the City of David at Jerusalem and realized that the city was built on a very steep hillside, with the palace on top of the hill. All the other houses would have been built descending from that place. It would have been easy for David to go full Peeping Tom whenever he wanted to.

So David is smitten by this hottie, and he asks around to find out who she is. Turns out she's a married woman, but that's a mere trifle for a king, so he invites her over and they . . . uh . . . do things. She commits adultery with David, and lo and behold becomes pregnant by him. This is obviously a major problem because her husband is not around, so David takes things to an even darker place. He sets it up for her husband, Uriah, to be killed in battle. Once he's dead, David marries her.

Let's pause to get this straight. David commits adultery, then covers it up by murdering the husband of the woman he's having an adulterous affair with. Sounds like a Lifetime movie, not something that God's chosen golden boy would ever do. Sometimes when I read the Bible, I'm amused by God's under-stated way of communicating. Second Samuel 11:27 gives a simple yet loaded summation of God's feelings about all this: "But the thing that David had done displeased the LORD" (NKJV). You think?

God sends the prophet Nathan to David, and using a clever little story, the prophet gives David a raw view of how horrible David's sin was against Uriah. God then drops the hammer on David—exactly what I think we all expect when He calls out our sin. But His true nature is also quite revealing even in His rebuke of David.

> I anointed you king over Israel, and I delivered you from the hand of Saul. I gave you your master's house and your master's wives into your keeping, and gave you the house of Israel and Judah. And if that had been too little, I also would have given you much more! Why have you despised the commandment of the LORD, to do evil in His sight? (2 Sam. 12:7–9 NKJV)

Make no mistake, God is ticked off right now. But even in His anger, He lets on that His heart is to bless David. "If that wasn't enough, I would have given you much more . . ." God loves to bless His friends, especially those whose hearts are to do His will and walk in obedience. But David chose sin over God's will, and there are always consequences to our disobedience. David probably should have been stripped of his kingship and, according to the laws God had set up in the old covenant, he probably should have been put to death. But then God tells David that He has "put away his sin." He is forgiving him. That being said, the consequences are steep.

David ruined a family, and now his family is going to be ruined. Evil will be raised up against David from within his own house, and he's going to have to deal with some pretty rotten kids in the future. And because David has done something so abhorrent to God, the son he conceived with Bathsheba is going to die.

God's grace covers even the worst of our sins, but consequences are still in play.

Most people stop paying attention to the story at this point. It seems like a solid ending to the ultimate cautionary tale. Don't mess with God because He sees all and vengeance will be His; what's done in the dark will be brought to the light, no matter who you are. And we turn and tiptoe away, examine our own sin issues, and gulp.

That's how I always dealt with this story. That is, until I read the whole thing and had a better understanding of God's heart, particularly for His friends. Sure enough, David's son is born and becomes ill almost immediately. David probably knows what's about to happen, yet he still fasts and prays day and night, because he also knows the nature of God. *Perhaps He will relent. Perhaps He will have mercy on my boy.*

But then the child dies, and instead of wailing and punching walls, David washes up and—worships? It is here we begin to really see the make of the man. David understands that God is holy and just, and no matter what happens, He deserves our praise. After David worships, he finally sits down to eat. Then, and this is an important detail, he comforts Bathsheba. The two drown their sorrows in each other. Through this "comforting," Bathsheba becomes pregnant again. Based on the timing, I think it is a safe assumption that the very night God's justice hit David, His mercy followed right behind it. God's desire is never for us to wallow in our wretchedness, to beat ourselves up or to hide in shame and guilt. His ultimate desire is to bless His friends, and in this story it is almost as if He can't wait to get back to the blessing as soon as the consequences are meted out.

One final detail cannot be overlooked. Second Samuel 12:24

goes out of its way to make an interesting point: "So she bore a son, and he called his name Solomon. Now the LORD loved him" (NKJV). His mother was an adulterer. His father the same, as well as a murderer. He was conceived through tragedy born out of treachery. Yet God loved him.

There truly is hope for all of us.

/4/

WHAT THE HELL?

Growing up in church, there were always a few constants.

- *You gotta be as good as you possibly can.* For me, this simply meant being polite and nice and making sure the bad things I did never got out in the open.
- *You gotta believe the right stuff.* You're a sinner. Jesus died for you. His resurrection broke sin and death's power. Jesus is the only way to God. The Bible is the Word of God. Agree with these statements and you are good to go.
- *The goal is salvation.* Believing in Jesus was important in that it saved me from hell. I mean, with hell on the table, I *had* to believe in Jesus. The alternative was an eternity of torture. No thanks, amigo. I'll take heaven, even if it means I'll have to spend eternity in church. I just hoped there would be some free time in heaven, because I wasn't sure I could worship nonstop forever.

The idea of hell was always a horizon issue for me. I was pretty sure I wasn't going to go there when I died, but I think I said the sinner's prayer for salvation a solid dozen times over the years, just to make absolutely certain I was in. So I never thought much about it until I started making these crazy movies. The backlash for my films has been interesting to watch (all I want to do is show the world how awesome God is), because almost all of it comes from fellow Christians, and the vast majority of their vitriol is about hell. Let me explain.

I've had a few face-to-face encounters with fellow Christians whose view of how we should "reach" non-Christians is diametrically opposed to my own. My first real foray into this debate was when I was filming my third movie, *Father of Lights*. I was trying to make a movie about who the Father is—His personality and character—and I was filming in Venice Beach, California. I am always looking for funky, interesting backdrops to film God doing God stuff, and Venice Beach is about as funky as it gets. It's a wonderland of countercultural misfits, profanity-laced T-shirts, and marijuana repositories, with a dash of straight-up lunacy thrown in.

The goal this day was to film with Doug Addison, who I discovered had a pretty unique gifting to use people's tattoos to prophesy over them. My movies are all about pushing boundaries, and I was hoping at the very least this could provide some interesting encounters that might lead to even more interesting discussions.

So we showed up and started walking along the boardwalk when I noticed a bunch of people holding up big yellow signs with Bible verses or other short statements on them. Some were speaking into megaphones, but most just stood there holding up their signs like tiny billboards. The signs said things like, "Sin Brings God's Wrath," "Repent and Believe," and "After Death, the Judgment." They weren't really talking to anyone, they just stood there. I approached one of the men holding a sign that said, "God Will Judge the World" and started a conversation. I honestly wanted to know what their mindset was. Did they really think they were doing any good?

The conversation was polite, but it became clear very early on that we had a major difference of opinion on how best to tell people about Jesus. When I asked the man if he thought it might be a little more effective to love people instead of holding up a sign, he responded with, "This is loving them. Telling them the truth. That's the most loving thing you can do." Okay. I mostly agreed with that. But the issue was, which truth are you going to tell them? There are really two sides, and both sides seem pretty entrenched in their philosophy.

One side says we need to show people God's love because it is His kindness that leads man to repentance (Rom. 2:4). The other side says we need to warn people that if they don't repent, they are going to hell (Luke 10:13–15). Both are true. The question isn't about who's right or wrong, but rather which approach is more effective. I mean, isn't that the point of all this anyway?

Another encounter with a critic of mine crystallized the difference between the two sides even more. I would often take my new films out on tour across the country, showing them in churches or large venues, sometimes including a concert or worship band. One of these events was at Rocketown in Nashville, and I was in the green room getting ready when someone walked in and told me there were protestors outside who were bugging everyone.

Protestors? Really? I mean, I knew some people didn't like my films, but this was the first time people had gone out of their way to show up at a venue and shout it from the rooftops. Having never been protested before, I wanted to meet them, so I walked outside to see what was up.

They weren't hard to find. They had set up shop in the corner of the parking lot and were on a bullhorn shouting out every Bible verse available about false teachers and how the Devil will masquerade as an angel of light and how a perverse generation seeks after signs and wonders. They also had huge, disgusting photographs of aborted fetuses, which didn't make much sense to me. We've never dealt with abortion in our films, but I just figured maybe there was a "protesting package" they put together to make sure they covered all their bases. There was a long line of people waiting to get into the venue, and while most were politely ignoring them, their bullhorn was so loud that it was very unpleasant.

I walked up to the guy on the bullhorn and extended my hand.

"Hi, I'm Darren."

The guy looked at me, then down at my hand, then back at me. He didn't shake my hand.

"I know who you are. You lie to people."

I was honestly surprised by this.

"I do?"

"Yes, you don't tell people they're going to hell if they don't repent."

"Ah," I replied, "well, I guess I just prefer to tell people how much God loves them instead."

We talked a little bit longer until it became clear this guy had no interest in any kind of honest dialogue, so I left him to head back inside. He picked up right where he had left off, and that was that. Oh, and we had a wonderful time showing the film that night, and many people gave their lives to the Lord or rededicated their lives back to Him. I'm not sure when the protestors left, but I'm pretty sure they felt great about having "told people the truth" about my films.

As much as I don't like to use the fear of hell to try to scare people into a decision for Christ, I readily admit that I fully believe in hell as a real place, and that the consequences of our sin, if left undealt with, will be horrific. I know there is a new movement of people questioning the reality of hell, but again, I tend to take Jesus at His word when I read the Scriptures. I also don't think we have much of a clue of what *really* happens when we die.

I read Rob Bell's controversial book *Love Wins* a few years back. In it he makes the argument against a literal hell, and I honestly enjoyed the book. To me it wasn't a hard-core denouncement of hell as much as one man's wrestling match with God about some uncomfortable things he was trying to work through. But unfortunately, many Christians didn't see it that way, because we don't want our Christian leaders questioning things. It confuses people (sigh).

This discussion has led many, including myself, to begin questioning things we've previously taken for granted. Hell was just hell. Accept Jesus for your get-out-of-jail-free card. But again, it was always about being saved *from* something as opposed to being saved *into* something.

Perhaps it's because I was unhappy in my Christian walk for so long that I immediately gravitate to the "saved into" camp. Getting saved from hell was mostly fear based, and it never ushered me into a deeper relationship with Jesus. It just got me out of punishment. But even Jesus rarely used this fear-based approach. His go-to statement—in fact, his very first public statement—was, "Repent, for the kingdom of heaven is at hand." Notice, it wasn't, "Repent, for the kingdom of hell is at hand." The kingdom of heaven, God's kingdom, is ready for the taking because of Jesus' sacrifice.

Focusing on hell may scare some people so much that they turn to Jesus, but usually what follows is an emptiness, because again, you're simply getting saved *from* a horrible place. What's the next step? Hopefully they find a good church and figure it out. But who knows? When you repent so you can join God's kingdom, you're stepping into something. You're entering a kingdom with a king, and you're joining a family. You are a son or daughter of the King and are privy to all the rights and privileges that go along with that. For me, the empowerment of entering a family far outweighed the relief of someplace horrible.

But there's a little more to all this than just the *idea* of hell. I, along with many others, have struggled with the idea of a loving Father sending His kids away forever to be tortured because they didn't believe in someone they couldn't see. This, more than anything, is what I've heard brought against God, and to be honest, I understand where they're coming from. "How could a loving God send people to hell simply for lack of belief?" It's a good question, but as with all these objections, to dwell on this is to miss the point.

Whenever this idea of God throwing people into hell is brought up, the visual that's conjured is of a dispassionate supreme being doling out a particular brand of justice in which He hurls the unfortunates into a boiling lake of lava where they'll never die but just burn in pain forever. This, I think, comes from the scene in Revelation 20:11–15:

> Then I saw a great white throne and him who was seated on it. From his presence earth and sky fled away, and no place was found for them. And I saw the dead, great and small, standing before the throne, and books were opened. Then another book was opened, which is the book of life. And the dead were judged by what was written in the books, according to what they had done. And the sea gave up the dead who were in it, Death and Hades gave up the dead who were in them, and they were judged, each one of them, according to what they had done. Then Death and Hades were thrown into the lake of fire. This is the second death, the lake of fire. And if anyone's name was not found written in the book of life, he was thrown into the lake of fire.

Yup, sounds pretty horrible. But here's the thing—it hasn't happened yet. A day will come when judgment comes for the living and the dead, when the ferocity of God's holiness says *enough is enough.* If you don't have a healthy fear of God, then you're in for a very rude awakening. Yes, He is love, but He is also God, ruler of heaven and earth, and He hates sin. And while that aspect of Him is present now, in His mercy He holds it back while He pursues all His children to turn to Him, to believe in His Son, and to have a relationship with Him.

I have no idea what hell is going to be like. I have no idea if there will be a literal lake of fire. I have no idea if that lake of fire (if it's literal) will simply be the end of a soul or if that soul will exist in that state for eternity. From a logical standpoint, I'm not sure I buy the whole idea of hell being a place where human souls are tortured by demons—because hell wasn't designed for us in the first place. It was designed for Satan and his demons! They're the ones who are going to feel the full wrath of God on that day, as Revelation 20:10 says, "And the devil who had deceived them was thrown into the lake of fire and sulfur, where the beast and the false prophet were, and they will be tormented day and night forever and ever" (NRSV). Yeah, Devil gonna get his.

It's hard to say with utter certainty what hell is going to be like, but there is one certainty we *do* know about hell, and it's the worst certainty of all. God. Jesus. The Holy Spirit. They won't be there. What will it be like for people to finally glimpse the full glory, majesty, righteousness, and love of God, and then realize they will never be able to be in His presence or look upon His glory or feel His loving-kindness again? Cut off from His presence, cut off from grace, cut off from mercy, cut off from love. There will be no love in hell. No hope. And quite honestly, that's far worse than any torment or physical pain. That's spiritual pain, and when I think of that I can begin to understand why there will be weeping and gnashing of teeth in hell. If everything that is good and pure and holy is gone, then all you are left with is a wasteland of death, decay, and hopelessness.

We know that hell, whatever it consists of, is going to be a royal suckfest. But we're still stuck with the objection of a loving God sending people there. And if it's for all eternity, it doesn't seem like the punishment fits the crime. An eternity of hell for fifty to seventy years of bad choices here on earth? That doesn't seem like justice; it feels like overkill.

Okay, so let's find our baseline going into this conversation. We may think we're smart, but in reality we are like small children trying to understand advanced physics. There are things at play we will never understand until we experience them, at which point it *will* all make sense to us. So while we're hopeless to be able to drill down to full and complete understanding, there are a few things in our childlike cubby holes that we can understand and hold onto when dealing with something as tricky and problematic as hell.

First, God is going to be the one doing the judging, not anyone else. And the brand of justice that God will dole out will be unlike anything we've ever seen before. First, He's definitely going to be fair to everyone: "And He will judge the world in righteousness; He will execute judgment for the peoples with equity" (Ps. 9:8 NASB). Second, He knows all: "There is no creature hidden from His sight, but all things are open and laid bare to [Him]" (Heb. 4:13 NASB). There are countless examples in our culture of people being falsely convicted of crimes, or of punishment being handed out not because of facts but because of prejudices or mistakes. That won't be the case on J-Day. The judgments will be so fair and righteous that no one will be able to argue against them. Including the accused.

I wonder if much of our problem is that while we want justice against people who do us wrong, none of us want judgment brought against us personally. If someone is sinning against us, we cry out for God to rain down His judgment on them. But if we're the ones sinning, we cry out for mercy. We no longer live in a culture where consequences for actions are highly valued. Everyone gets a trophy, no matter how they've performed. While the merits of this could be debated, a lack of consequences severely weakens the value of true accountability.

But even more than that, I think many people look at this

picture of God, arbitrary or not, saying "you're in, you're out" based on what people believed and what they did, and they see a cosmic bully rather than a wise, righteous judge. This used to be one of my core complaints about God, and I even had (I thought) the Bible verses to prove it. Check this baby out:

> For he says to Moses, "I will have mercy on whom I have mercy, and I will have compassion on whom I have compassion." So then it depends not on human will or exertion, but on God, who has mercy. For the Scripture says to Pharaoh, "For this very purpose I have raised you up, that I might show my power in you, and that my name might be proclaimed in all the earth." So then he has mercy on whomever he wills, and he hardens whomever he wills.
>
> You will say to me then, "Why does he still find fault? For who can resist his will?" But who are you, O man, to answer back to God? Will what is molded say to its molder, "Why have you made me like this?" Has the potter no right over the clay, to make out of the same lump one vessel for honorable use and another for dishonorable use? (Rom. 9:15–21)

When I was a teenager trying to figure out what I believed, I remember the first time I encountered those verses. I was in my room, reading my brand-new NIV Student Bible my parents had bought me (excited, no doubt, that their kid was actually showing some interest in God), and I was working my way through Romans when I hit that little gem. I remember the feeling of excitement I had as Paul was building the question, and the utter deflation that followed when, in essence, God pulled the "because I said so" card. It's a passage I still struggle with to some degree. It paints a picture that we're all just pawns in some cosmic game, and God is moving everything around, playing chess with Himself.

Well that's one way to look at it.

But there's another way as well.

Remember how, compared to God's infinite intelligence, we're all just toddlers trying to understand advanced physics? Maybe that "who are you, O man, to answer back to God" isn't meant as an old man shouting on his lawn, but is instead God reaching the end of what He can explain that will make any sense to us. We see the same thing happen in Job, when, at the end of it all, Job is letting God have it, wondering why this is all happening to him. And then, from Job 38 to basically the end of the book, the Lord unleashes on him. It's much too long to quote it all here, but for a good time, go check out Job 38–42. I'll point out a few juicy bits here.

You know you're in for it when God starts with, "Gird up your loins like a man, I will question you" (Job 38:3 NRSV). That's when you know you've lost before the conversation even begins. God then goes on an epic diatribe in which He asks Job where he was while God was busy creating and running the entire universe. This rebuttal leaves Job dazed, and he's a beaten man when he responds:

> "Behold, I am of small account; what shall I answer you?
>> I lay my hand on my mouth.
> I have spoken once, and I will not answer;
>> twice, but I will proceed no further." (Job 40:3–5)

I love this response. It's basically Job admitting, "Well, shoot. I never should have opened my mouth. I'm done talking now." But God isn't done yet—He's just getting warmed up. God's next

CHASING A GOD YOU DON'T WANT TO CATCH

bit hits to the heart of the matter in Job's thinking, and indeed, in the thinking behind what we're dealing with in this chapter. Listen to this:

> "Dress for action like a man;
>> I will question you, and you make it known to me.
> Will you even put me in the wrong?
>> Will you condemn me that you may be in the right?"
> (Job 40:7–8)

God is asking Job, "Are you going to say I'm not righteous and holy? Are you, by your puny logic, going to condemn Me, call Me a bully and a tyrant, so that you are more righteous than Me?" This is why I cringe whenever I hear an atheist use the argument that they have a "moral obligation not to believe in God, because if He's real, then He's a horrible person for letting bad things happen in the world when He has the power to stop them." Anyone who thinks they are more righteous, loving, or merciful than God is not thinking straight. Do you really want to condemn God so that you seem like you're in the right morally? Good luck with that.

God hammers the point home to Job once again, and by the end Job is completely humbled. Man, I can't imagine what he must have felt like, being on the wrong end of that argument. You can tell God was hot, almost as if He was getting out all His frustrations from generations of His kids leveling the same charges of unfairness and evil at Him. Job's response is, well, he just gives up.

> Then Job answered the Lord and said:
> "I know that you can do all things,

and that no purpose of yours can be thwarted.
'Who is this that hides counsel without knowledge?'
Therefore I have uttered what I did not understand,
    things too wonderful for me, which I did not know.
'Hear, and I will speak;
    I will question you, and you make it known to me.'
I had heard of you by the hearing of the ear,
    but now my eye sees you;
therefore I despise myself,
    and repent in dust and ashes." (Job 42:1–6)

Job's response is where I've ended up, minus the tongue lashing from God. "I have uttered what I did not understand, things too wonderful for me, which I did not know." Isn't that the crux of all this? We think we're so smart, that we understand so much, that we're the superior moral beings in the universe, but at the end of the day even the smartest among us are worms compared to God's understanding. Some things are just above our pay grade.

THE INVISIBLE COMPLEXITY

I love to watch documentaries of nature, like the *Planet Earth* series, where an entire subset of our world is shown to me—one I never knew existed. The beauty and complexity of the world around me is mind-blowing. And then I'll sometimes watch a special on space or quantum physics or microbiology, and the complexity of creation becomes almost overwhelming. There are layers upon layers of the world and matter we cannot see. From microorganisms to atoms to cells to plants to ultraviolet rays, it goes on seemingly forever.

But what has brought me much comfort is the idea that God created *both* the heavens and the earth. We're quick to be impressed with His earth—with the creation we can see with our eyes—but what about His heavens? I don't think He's talking about just a place called heaven here but another world entirely. There is a physical world, yes, but there is also a spiritual world. And wouldn't it make sense that God's spiritual world would be just as incredible and complex and mind-numbingly vast as His physical world?

Maybe, just maybe, there is as much happening in the invisible spiritual world as is happening here in the physical one. Maybe God's judgments don't just take into account what we do in the physical world but also what is happening simultaneously in this vast, complicated, unseen spiritual world.

God has promised that His judgments will be pure, honest, and holy. His judgments will be perfect, because He will have all the facts, all the circumstances, and all the data from our hearts, our minds, and our actions.

But there is one more important thing we have to think about, and it is perhaps the most important factor of all.

If God is real, then there are only two possible ways He runs this joint. Either He's the puppet master, causing people to do this or that, and is basically playing chess with Himself, or He has truly decided to give His creation total freedom to do whatever they want to do. Obviously, I'm in the freedom camp, because you can never have true love without freedom. If God were controlling everyone, it would be the equivalent of placing a computer program inside us or hardwiring us to get to some inevitable conclusion that He wants. That would mean that our love for God and our choosing of Him in our lives is not love at all, but subtle manipulation of circumstances to reach a pre-determined outcome.

But 1 John 4:8 tells us explicitly that "God is love," and 1 Corinthians 13 lays out exactly how that love functions. The death blow to the "God is controlling everyone" argument comes in 1 Corinthians 13:5: "(Love) does not insist on its own way." This means that God never insists on having His own way when dealing with us, because He has given us true freedom to choose or reject Him, to live holy or sinful lives.

As my good friend Bryan Schwartz likes to say, "God honors choice." He will try to make it very difficult for you to ultimately not want to choose Him, but if that's truly what you desire, then He's not going to stop you from getting what you want. And really, hell is just God giving people what they want. You want an existence without God in your life? Well okay, here you go.

If hell were just a place of torture, it would be horrific, but it wouldn't be hell. Hell is only *hell* because God is gone. And if God is gone, that means all His attributes are gone as well. Maybe there isn't any fire or brimstone at all in hell, maybe the demons who were supposed to be torturing you are all being tortured themselves in a lake of fire. Maybe you and millions of others just exist in some place. But there will be no love, no kindness, no mercy, no grace, no forgiveness, no law, no justice, no warmth, no purity, no humility, no hope. Forget what the surroundings are—torture or no torture—that really isn't what makes it hellish. It's the absence of God that will bring about the weeping and gnashing of teeth.

In the world today, those who reject God's love for themselves can still experience the attributes of God because He permeates His creation. God "makes his sun rise on the evil and on the good, and sends rain on the just and on the unjust" (Matt. 5:45). The choice is yours for your entire conscious existence in this world. You can either say, "Yes, I want to receive God's love, forgiveness, and grace," or you can say, "Nah, I'm good on my own." Whatever you choose, God will honor it.

God's invisibility is still frustrating to me. I hear the argument in my own head: "But God, you've hidden yourself almost too well for most people! They can't see or feel you, and it's hard for people to believe in something they can never see. And then, when the end finally comes, we'll all see you, and at that point those who never saw and didn't believe will obviously want to receive your love because for the first time they'll be able see it, but you won't let them. You'll say, 'Too bad, it's too late for you. You should have believed in the invisible me.'" It just doesn't seem fair.

But the Bible deals with even this objection! In Luke 16, Jesus has another storytime session with His disciples where He lays it all out for them. He tells them a parable about two guys who couldn't be more different in life. One is mega rich, lives in the lap of luxury, and doesn't care about anyone but himself. The other is a poor beggar who lives outside the gate of the rich man's estate, hoping to just glean a little sustenance from the garbage the guy throws out. At some point both men die, and the rich guy goes to hell while the poor man goes to heaven. The rich guy cries out for just a drop of water, just an ounce of goodness in this godless place, but it's not going to happen. He then says:

"Then I beg you, father, to send him to my father's house—for I have five brothers—so that he may warn them, lest they also come into this place of torment." But Abraham said, "They have Moses and the Prophets; let them hear them." And he said, "No, father Abraham, but if someone goes to them from the dead, they will repent." He said to him, "If they do not hear Moses and the Prophets, neither will they be convinced if someone should rise from the dead." (Luke 16:27–31)

The dead rich guy sees the error of his ways, but there's nothing he can do about it. So he requests what we skeptics see as logical. *Send the poor guy to my family to warn them so they don't wind up in hell like me.* Abraham counters that they have Moses and the prophets—they have the Word of God—at their immediate disposal. All they have to do is believe. And that's when the rich man says: "If someone goes to them from the dead, then they'll believe." Send them a ghost, something supernatural, something they can *see*. Then they'll believe because they can see something.

But Abraham counters with, "Look, if their hearts were open to God, then Moses and the prophets would be more than enough." God understands the human heart way more than we ever will. We all have those people in our lives who are not living in a godly way, or who are making destructive decisions that God's Word makes clear are a path to nowhere good. And we think if only God would show them this or that in a very particular way, then they would see the light and repent and get with the program. But as Jesus shows in this parable, this is a false hope, based on our limited understanding of the human heart and mind.

Jesus says, "If any man have ears to hear, let him hear," eight times. There is a deep truth embedded in this phrase that we would be wise to pay attention to. When truth is presented, we have two options. We can either have ears to hear it, or we can choose to reject it. Jesus' use of the word *if* is a big one, because it means we have a real, viable choice in the matter.

What will you do when presented with the goodness of God and His desire to have an everlasting friendship with you? What will you do when you're confronted with biblical truth that doesn't line up with your personal desires? What choice will you make? Will you have ears to hear God's desire for your life, or will you try to figure out ways to finagle God and Scripture to fit into the lifestyle you want instead?

When I was at my lowest spiritually, and my family was constantly praying for me to wake up, I had countless opportunities to choose God. But I never did. Why? This is the God's honest truth: I didn't want to. I didn't want to give my life over to God, didn't want to have to deal with my sin.

I have vivid memories of church services, conferences, and special speakers who rattled my soul, then offered the opportunity to do something about what I'd just heard. And I always sat quietly in my seat because I didn't want to do it. I knew I should, knew it would be good for me, but I *chose* to say no. It was 100 percent my own decision. I wanted to stay where I was, as I was, because I was frightened of change. Frightened of exposure. Frightened of God.

While some may still see the idea of hell and judgment as something "morally bad" that God engages in, it all comes down to each person making choices. Life is a journey that must be respected. Along this journey we will make thousands, even millions, of choices for which we will be accountable. Judgment isn't a reckoning as much as a finite point in time when the journey of choice is over and the sum of all our choices is respected.

Welcome to existence.

/5/

IT'S TIME FOR A SPANKING

When I was a kid, our family had a dark orange chair that was the equivalent of the French Bastille in the 1700s. Whenever I did something really wrong, I would be told to go sit in the orange chair to await my sentencing. A trip to the orange chair was a one-way ticket to Painville. I knew what was coming, and there would be no escape. I could only sit there, hoping beyond hope that my judge would be Mom and not Dad. Mom was a softy, you see, and her spankings were halfhearted at best. But Dad . . . well, Dad was another story. He was a potter, and his powerful forearms turned an ordinary wooden spoon into a weapon of mass destruction for my rear end.

Apparently we're not allowed to spank kids anymore, but back in the day that orange chair got some work. And while the spankings themselves were bad, they were always over pretty quickly. Three solid whacks and it was done. I'd be wailing and wriggling to get away while my parents tried to hug me, telling me some nonsense about how this hurt them more than it hurt me. Yeah, right. Tell that to my throbbing butt.

But the moment before the actual punishment was doled out was the absolute worst. I knew what was coming, and the wait was agony. I can still remember my whole body clenching up in the seconds before the first whack came. This was punishment for doing something bad. And punishment always hurt. It didn't take long for my kid brain to realize that I needed to avoid punishment at all costs.

I have other memories of punishment as well, and while many of them didn't involve physical pain, they were almost worse than a quick thump on my backside. I was always a pretty good kid (mostly because I hated being punished!) and I rarely got into trouble. But every once in a while trouble would find me. One time, in fifth grade, two kids got in a shoving match in the hallway of our Lutheran elementary school, and it was escalating quickly. I'm not sure what came over me, but before I knew it I was smack in the middle of the fracas, doing my best to try to break it up. I got shoved around until I felt a forceful hand on my arm and the unmistakable strength of a teacher pulling me out of it. The whole class was there, staring at us. I didn't like this feeling. I felt uncovered in some way, even though I knew I hadn't done anything wrong. But all eyes were on me.

When the teacher told us all to report to the principal's office, I tried to protest that I was just trying to break up the fight, but the teacher didn't want to hear it. So we marched off like POWs, and for the first time in my life I found myself in the principal's office—the stuff of legends for a fifth grader. He wasn't there yet, so the three of us sat in silence, knowing certain doom was looming.

When he entered the room, his face was serious. He asked what happened, and I explained that I was just trying to break up the fight. Even though I was terrified, I also knew in my heart that I hadn't done anything wrong. Still, this was the fifth-grade equivalent of prison, and I just wanted to get out of there. After hearing our stories, we received our punishment. No recess. He might as well have just stuck a dagger in my heart. To take away a kid's recess was to take away his will to live. It didn't matter that I was trying to break up the fight; I was busted just like the other two. It was a foul day indeed.

Sitting in that principal's office just reenforced my desire to never, ever get into trouble again. I hated that feeling and the premonition of doom. I remember the various troublemaker kids throughout my time in grade school and on through high school. I watched in amazement as they did things that brought swift consequences, yet they never seemed fazed. Now I realize that their home lives were probably train wrecks and they were filled with anger, sadness, and an overall sense of helplessness, so lashing out at the system was their only way to gain some semblance of control, but back then all I saw were kids my age willfully courting the punishment I so desperately wanted to avoid. I couldn't relate to them at all. It was as if they were another species of kid entirely.

It should come as no surprise that I carried this deep desire to avoid punishment into my relationship with God. If anything, this was an infinitely worse prospect than any principal's office or wooden spoon. God's punishment was unstoppable and could come in almost limitless forms. He was invisible, so you'd never see it coming, and there was absolutely no hiding from Him. Everyone else thought I was a great kid, but God knew the real truth. He knew I was a liar. He knew my thought life. He knew how little I truly loved others. He knew all my dirty little secrets, and it was only a matter of time before He would appear out of nowhere with a reckoning that would bring pain and shame in swift order.

What do you do when the God you're supposed to love above all others is also the one who is most likely to make your life miserable? My solution was the same one that's been used by countless millions since the very beginning. I would try to hide from Him. Of course, hiding from God is impossible, but for me hiding took the form of keeping Him at a safe distance.

Remember, I actually read the Bible. I saw how He treated His friends. Like Uncle Ben told Spider-Man, with great power comes great responsibility, and that seemed to hold true with God's friends. The closer they got to God, the higher the stakes. Why would anyone willfully do that to themselves? So I purposely avoided going "all in" with God, because that way very little would be expected of me. I believed all the right things, had dotted my i's and crossed my t's, so I knew I was getting in to heaven. Why risk the wrath of God by getting too close to Him? I mean, just look at this verse: "Not many of you should become teachers, my fellow believers, because you know that we who teach will be judged more strictly" (James 3:1 NIV).

And that is precisely my point! The closer you get, the more you know, the smaller the window of mercy gets, apparently. No thank you. Best to just be a religious doofus so the expectations on your life will be next to nothing.

I thought I had loads of proof for what I believed about God doling out punishment in extra doses to those He was closest to from the Bible, but in my journey to intimate friendship with

Him, I slowly began to realize that I had been looking at these stories all wrong. As in all things with God, faith is a two-way street, and to ignore the part we play in our stories is to miss a crucial element of truth.

THE HUMBLEST EVER?

It's no secret that I have something of a biblical man-crush on Moses. This guy is everything I want to be when I grow up. Well, minus the killing a guy part, the hiding out in the wilderness for forty years part, the begging God not to choose him part—actually I just really want the best friends with God part.

You know the story—you've all seen *The Prince of Egypt*. The Hebrew people are getting crushed by the Egyptians because there are simply too many of them for Egypt's liking, and Moses narrowly escapes the mandated genocide of Hebrew newborns because of his quick-witted sister. He gets taken into the house of Pharaoh and lives a posh, charmed life until he sees an Egyptian taskmaster beating two Hebrews. Moses decides to brandish his own kind of justice and kills the Egyptian like some biblical Clint Eastwood. He thought nobody saw, but of course they did, and he has to take off on the run and lives in exile for the next forty years or so. Then a burning bush talks to him.

Can we just pause here to contemplate something? This is another reason I never wanted to get too involved with God, because it seemed like everyone who became a part of God's posse had some kind of crazy, weird, or powerful encounter with Him. And I never did—well, not until I did. But even more than that, I wasn't sure I *wanted* to have one of these encounters with

God. After all, they were pretty weird. And I was never a big fan of weird.

I love how we read our Bibles and take everything in them as if it's a ho-hum walk on the beach. A bush that talks? Sure, why not? The bush is burning but not burning up? Okay, sounds good. Over the years I've learned to hear the voice of God pretty well for myself, and just like Elijah's experience, it almost always comes as a whisper, and sometimes even a whisper of a whisper! I'm usually fairly sure I heard something from God, but then again, I can never be fully certain. I just have to take it on faith and hope I heard correctly. But these biblical fellas, they get, like, Broadway show tunes in their introductions to the Lord.

With Moses it gets even weirder though. Not only does he get some talking shrubbery, but the Lord puts on a kind of magic show for him. But before we get to that, let's talk about why God needs to do this and what it might teach us about true friendship with God.

When Moses approaches the burning bush, God tells him to remove his sandals because he's standing on holy ground. Why is it holy? Because God is there. This conversation, this whole scene, is going to go down as one of the most important conversations in human history. The plagues of Egypt. The Passover. The parting of the Red Sea. The Ten Commandments. So much important biblical history is on its way, but it all starts with this moment between a man running from his past and a God who, for whatever reason, chose that man to be His mouthpiece. Moses has no idea how important all this is going to be, but God does. God just needs His man to sign on the dotted line of destiny.

God lays it out nice and clear. The Hebrew people are crying out to Him for help, and He has heard their cry. It's time to rescue

His chosen people from oppression. *It's you, Moses, whom I have chosen to go speak to Pharaoh and bring my people out of Egypt. It's time to stop tending sheep and become the greatest liberator the world has ever seen.*

That's a pretty good promotion. But of course, Moses is just like you and me. He's just a man with skeletons in his closet and no great desire to upend his comfy life. So his reply isn't no, per se, but he clearly wants nothing to do with this assignment. "Who am I that I should go to Pharaoh and bring the children of Israel out of Egypt?" (Ex. 3:11). You've got the wrong guy, God. Obviously.

But God knows He has the right guy, so He assures Moses that He will be with him, and He even tells Moses He'll give him a sign to prove it . . . someday. "But I will be with you, and this shall be the sign for you, that I have sent you: when you have brought the people out of Egypt, you shall serve God on this mountain" (Ex. 3:12). If all God does to prove Himself to Moses is done in this particular moment, then it really *is* just a magic trick. But God is always interested in relationship, and, true to form, He plants a seed here that will sprout later in Exodus 19.

Moses essentially asks the Lord, "Who am I supposed to tell them sent me?" I always read this and scratched my head. Duh, Moses, it's God. But then I realized that Moses has no idea who God is at this point. He grew up in Pharaoh's palace, where they worshiped many gods. So not only is this a key moment in history, it's a get-to-know-you sesh.

God, realizing He's going to have to hold Moses' hand a bit while this all sinks in, gives Moses His business card to show to the Hebrew leaders in Egypt. They'll at least know who Moses is talking about. Then God basically lays out the whole plot for

Moses so there are no surprises. *First you'll say this, then he'll respond this way, then I'll drop some God-style bombs on them, and not only will they let you go, but they're going to pay you on your way out.*

This is when Moses learns his first lesson about friendship with God. For many people, experiencing a talking plant and having the whole scenario laid out for them would probably be enough. They'd say, "Okay, what do I do now?" But not Moses. No, Moses pushes back: "But behold, they will not believe me or listen to my voice, for they will say, 'The LORD did not appear to you'" (Ex. 4:1).

Now please hear me. I'm not saying we should emulate the part when Moses pushes back on what God is asking him to do. No, it's the humanity Moses shows, the vulnerability. When God told Moses who He was, Moses hid his face because he realized he was talking to God Himself. I don't think Moses was being a coward or cheeky; I think he was being bluntly honest about not feeling up to this enormous task. We see glimpses of this same thing later when Moses pushes back on God wanting to destroy the whole lot of ungrateful people. Moses wasn't an argumentative guy, but he was one who would tell God the truth of his heart.

Why is this a big deal? I'm willing to admit that I have often struggled with trying to put on a happy, churchy face with God when deep inside I'm a hot mess of insecurities, doubts, fears, and anger. Maybe it's the fake church sheen I grew up with, or maybe it's just me attempting to ignore my own issues long enough, hoping that they'll just go away. Whatever it is, this lack of honesty with God and myself does nothing to further my relationship with Him. If anything, it puts up a wall between us. After all, God already knows me better than I know myself.

We all have different levels of friends. Some friends are merely acquaintances—people you see once in a while and your conversations are light and mostly happy. You talk about the weather, kids, sports, your job, whatever. Other friends are "real" friends in the sense that they know the hardships you've gone through, some of the struggles you've had with family and relationships, and a few things that go beyond normal chitchat. But then you have those deep, "best" friendships. These are the people who know your innermost secrets, know you at both your best and your worst, yet still choose to stick by you. These are the friendships we guard with our lives. And this is the kind of friendship I want to have with my God. But the only way I can do that is to admit things to Him that I don't want to admit to myself. I have to confess things to Him that are embarrassing, shameful, and sometimes even evil. The wonderful thing about the Lord, though, is no matter what, He will never leave or forsake me. Never.

At their first meeting, Moses doesn't try to put on a false face for God. He opens up right away and admits that he is not up for this job, that he thinks God has the wrong guy. He's thinking this through, and he realizes that he's going to be some nobody walking in saying God talked to him through a burning bush and, well, that just sounds crazy. They'll never believe him. And that's when God goes full David Copperfield on him.

> The Lord said to him, "What is that in your hand?" He said, "A staff." And he said, "Throw it on the ground." So he threw it on the ground, and it became a serpent, and Moses ran from it. But the Lord said to Moses, "Put out your hand and catch it by the tail"—so he put out his hand and caught it, and it became

a staff in his hand—"that they may believe that the LORD, the
God of their fathers, the God of Abraham, the God of Isaac,
and the God of Jacob, has appeared to you." (Ex. 4:2–5)

See, this is the stuff I'm talking about. Who gets this kind
of introduction to God? Throw your staff on the ground and it
turns into a snake?! But God doesn't stop there—He then has
Moses put his hand in his cloak to turn it leprous and then back
to normal again. And as if *that's* not enough, God tells Moses
that if He needs to pull out a showstopper, go ahead and pour
some water from the Nile (a sacred river for the Egyptians) on
dry ground and God will turn it into blood. This is some serious
God stuff going on, and I'm pretty sure it would be more than
enough for the average human to do what God says. But Moses
isn't average, apparently, and he has one more excuse to try.

"Oh, my Lord, I am not eloquent, either in the past or since
you have spoken to your servant, but I am slow of speech and of
tongue" (Ex. 4:10). This guy has just experienced enough signs
and wonders to last most people a lifetime of speaking gigs and
at least three book deals, but Moses has run *far* from his original
calling, and he's beyond reluctant to step back into it. So he goes
the old, "I'm not a good public speaker" route. To which God
replies: "Who has made man's mouth? Who makes him mute,
or deaf, or seeing, or blind? Is it not I, the LORD? Now therefore
go, and I will be with your mouth and teach you what you shall
speak" (Ex. 4:11–12).

Checkmate, Moses. You're all out of excuses now. And Moses
knows it, so his only recourse is to go the childish route: "Oh, my
Lord, please send someone else" (Ex. 4:13).

And here we get to the crux of Moses' problem. He flat-out

doesn't want to do this. He doesn't want to obey the Lord. And it is here where his wrestling with God crosses the line from honest vulnerability to outright disobedience. And disobedience is the big no-no if your goal is friendship with God. The result isn't pretty. "Then the anger of the LORD was kindled against Moses" (Ex. 4:14).

And there it is. "The anger of the LORD was kindled against Moses." That, folks, is not the place you ever want to be. God tells Moses that his brother Aaron can do the speaking, and He tells him to pick up his staff and go. Notice there is no response from Moses after this (Ex. 4:14–17). Just like Job, when the anger of the Lord is kindled because of your disobedience, you are reminded very quickly of your true place. God may want to be your friend, but He is not your buddy. You are not equals in any way. It is only through His mercy and kindness that He stoops to your level for love and relationship. He doesn't need you for anything, but He does *want* you.

Now that we've got this fairly inauspicious beginning of a friendship out of the way, let's fast-forward to where it all comes crashing down for Moses. To do so we need to jump past a lot of history that God and Moses build up together that brings them into a personal friendship unlike pretty much anything the world has seen before or since.

Moses, probably still smarting from that rebuke God gave him to get going, heads back to Egypt and confronts Pharaoh about letting the Hebrew people go. The whole deal turns into the first big blockbuster action movie, complete with blood water, frogs, gnats, locusts, and flies, an outbreak of boils (eww), a hailstorm for the ages, the sun going dark, and the angel of death being unleashed. This finally gets the Hebrews the hall pass they've been waiting for, and just as God said, the Egyptians are so freaked out that they give the Israelites their gold and jewelry on their way out of town.

But after a few days, Pharaoh changes his mind and goes after them with his army. Cue the parting of the Red Sea, the race to the other side, and the water closing. Then we've got manna showing up to feed everyone, water from a rock, the Ten Commandments, the law, and the most ungrateful group of people in the history of the world. They build the ark of the covenant that Indiana Jones will one day find, a moving tabernacle that will be God's chill pad, and a golden calf that is monumentally stupid. Then more grumbling and complaining as the Israelites realize this isn't going to be a glamping vacay but a straight-up life of survivalist wilderness training.

This leads to a mini-coup attempt by Aaron and his sister, Miriam, which does not go well for them. They're grumbling against Moses, believing they deserve a bigger piece of the pie because the Lord has spoken through them as well. This scene gives a glimpse of how far Moses and God have come in their friendship and also shows what it's like when God truly has your back.

Numbers 12:3 says, "Moses was the most humble person on the face of the earth." (How Moses wrote that with a straight face is beyond me.) We know humility is a big deal to God, and presumably Moses' friendship with God has shaped him into a man who knows God intimately. God "opposes the proud but shows favor to the humble" (1 Peter 5:5 NIV). A humble heart is one of the secret sauces to friendship with God. Remember, in God's kingdom everything is turned upside down. The greatest serve the weakest. Pride is so damaging because it pulls us out of the kingdom and elevates us internally to a position of superiority over the very brothers and sisters we are called to love and serve. Many church leaders and celebrities should take note. If you operate from a place of pride, God will not just remove favor from you, He will actively *oppose* you!

So God hears Aaron and Miriam bellyaching and, like a stern father, lets them know that He is very displeased. God explains that He speaks to everyone else in visions or dreams. But not Moses. "With him I speak mouth to mouth, clearly, and not in riddles, and he beholds the form of the LORD" (Num. 12:8). Moses' humble heart and dogged obedience (despite his rough start) have made this relationship into perhaps the best friendship with a human being that God has ever had. And He lets Aaron and Miriam know that they do not share that same kind of friendship with Him, so, you know, stop it.

This is where the relationship between God and Moses is when the big screwup happens. The gist of the story is simple. The people are near rebellion again, and Moses is in their crosshairs because there's no water where he's led them and they're convinced they're all going to die. So God tells Moses to speak to a rock before the people and God will draw water from it. They've already done this once before when God told Moses to strike the rock in front of the people and He'd bring water from it (Ex. 17:6). But this time, God tells Moses to *speak* to the rock and He'll bring water from it. Moses, unfortunately, calls an audible:

> Then Moses and Aaron gathered the assembly together before the rock, and he said to them, "Hear now, you rebels: shall we bring water for you out of this rock?" And Moses lifted up his hand and struck the rock with his staff twice, and water

came out abundantly, and the congregation drank, and their livestock. (Num. 20:10–11)

Speak to the rock this time, don't hit it. Moses instead does what worked last time, and that's it. He's out:

And the LORD said to Moses and Aaron, "Because you did not believe in me, to uphold me as holy in the eyes of the people of Israel, therefore you shall not bring this assembly into the land that I have given them." (Num. 20:12)

Think about everything Moses had done for the Lord leading up to this mistake. He'd taken on the most powerful ruler in the world, done crazy magic-show-like wonders, been a punching bag for the Israelites, taken a second job as a circuit court judge for disputes, and even talked God out of nuking the entire population because of their bad behavior. But make one tiny mistake with a seemingly inconsequential direction and *you're done*. You can no longer have your heart's desire of entering the promised land with the Israelites you led out of Egypt. *Now get back to work, Moses.*

That's how I always viewed this story, and it's why I was never going to allow myself to get too close to God. Sure He was "gracious and compassionate, slow to anger and abounding in love, and he relents from sending calamity" (Joel 2:13 NIV), but from stories like this, it seemed like the ones who got closest to Him faced the most calamity for the smallest infractions.

But then I had a conversation about this with my friend Philip Mantofa, an incredible pastor from Indonesia. He pointed out that this was not a punishment as much as it was a mercy. Let me explain.

What do we know about Moses at this point? He's gone through the fire with God in a big way and has moved the heart of God to the point that he is basically the first person since Adam who gets to speak to God face-to-face like a friend. His friendship with God is rooted in total obedience (which, remember, is simply faith) and a humble heart to the extreme. But right here, in the wilderness of some place called Meribah, all that is being threatened by two things. Disobedience and pride. If this rebellion of the heart goes unchecked, God is in very real danger of losing His friend.

Look at what Moses basically says: "What do I have to do . . ." Those are not the words of a humble heart. This is a man who, in his fear of the mob, wants them to understand that he is their savior of sorts. *You seriously want to question me, you rebels? You want me to show you what I'm made of, what kind of special standing with God I have? You need me to show you how powerful I am?* As if that wasn't bad enough, he then blatantly disregards God's command to speak to the rock in favor of the dramatic and dazzling display of using his magic staff to prove himself (not God) to them.

So he strikes the rock twice and water flows. This event never ceases to amaze me because it also reveals a hidden aspect of God's heart for His friends, even those walking in rebellion. God is love, and God loves His friends immensely. Scripture tells us Moses hit the rock twice, and then water came forth abundantly. Why twice? I wonder if it was God giving him a mulligan, as if He was asking Moses, *Are you sure you really want to do this?* Did Moses pause between strikes? Did he think for a second that maybe this wasn't such a good idea, but now he was too far into his sin to pull back? We'll never know, and it doesn't really matter, because he plowed ahead and hit it again.

Why water flowed from the rock at all is the bigger question. If I'm God in this situation, and my friend is leaving the reservation, I'm just going to sit back and watch him make a fool of himself. Hit the rock a hundred times, Moses, break your staff for all I care. You think it's you bringing water from that thing? Think again.

But God doesn't think like us, and His heart is infinitely more loving than we can ever comprehend. He doesn't tolerate sin, as is shown by the swift repercussions after Moses' little tantrum. But He apparently does continue to love us in the midst of our sin, even at our very worst and most ugly moments. This is Moses' low point, yet God is still with him, and because Moses is His friend, and God's nature is one of love, mercy, and patience, He acquiesces to Moses and lets him look like the savior he's selling to the people. God takes His friendships very seriously, even if we don't.

In his punishment, God makes it clear where the heart of the sin lies: "Because you did not believe in me" (Num. 20:12). Moses' pride, his not following orders is, at the root, a lack of faith in God. A lack of trust. Moses has just put the greatest friendship in world history at risk because he has undermined the very thing that binds that friendship together.

This is what my friend Philip meant when he explained to me that God's punishment was not as much punishment as it was mercy. As someone who has tasted true friendship with God, I can say categorically that my relationship with the Lord is the thing I hold most dear in all the world. More than my family, my kids, my accomplishments—they all pale in comparison to my desire to never lose the friendship I have with the Father. So I think I can rightly assume that his friendship with God was the dearest thing in Moses' heart as well, and he would give up almost anything to protect it. What God does, then, is give Moses a daily reminder of the DNA of their relationship. He will lead the people to a place he cannot go, and that knowledge will serve to keep Moses' heart where it needs to be for this friendship to continue.

But of course, like any good Father, at the end of the day God is a giant softy who loves to give His kids wonderful gifts, and it stands to reason that He wanted to bless Moses beyond his wildest dreams. Even though Moses made a grievous mistake and judgment was passed, God still found a way to circumvent His own decree.

In Luke 9, Jesus takes his three best buds up a mountain and gives them a sneak peek at His glory in the transfiguration. And who else shows up to hang with Jesus for a little chitchat but Elijah and . . . yup, Moses. God let him into the promised land anyway. And to top it off, on his first visit he gets to hang out with the Lord Himself and talk to Him face-to-face, just like old times.

/6/

WHAT WILL HE TAKE FROM ME?

It was supposed to be a heartfelt story. The person who first told it to me had the best intentions, but the effect it had on me was quite the opposite of what they were intending. Instead of showing me a picture of beautiful faith, it once again reinforced what I had secretly believed for years. That God was not on my side. If I gave Him my whole heart and held nothing back from Him, then He was going to do something to me that would ultimately test the strength of my conviction. He was going to take the thing I loved most away from me to prove a point.

Horatio Spafford was a successful lawyer and businessman from Chicago back in the day. He was married with five kids. In 1871, his son died of pneumonia and he lost most of his business to the Great Chicago Fire, but he dug his way out and recovered despite the loss. In 1873, an ocean liner carrying his wife and children struck another ship and sank, and only his wife remained alive. When Horatio heard from his wife that all their children had been killed, he booked a ticket on a ship the next day to head over to be with her. About four days into the voyage, the captain told Spafford that they were now at the spot where his children had died.

Spafford sat down and wrote the great hymn "It Is Well with My Soul," looking out at the exact spot of the ocean that had swallowed his children.

> *When peace like a river attendeth my way,*
> *When sorrows like sea billows roll,*
> *Whatever my lot, Thou has taught me to say,*
> *It is well, it is well with my soul.*

His wife, Anna, was quoted as saying, "God gave me four daughters. Now they have been taken from me. Someday I will understand why."

Every time I heard this story, the intention was to highlight the profound faith of Horatio Spafford. And for many I'm sure that's exactly how they experience it. But for me it was always a different reaction. My internal battle would ignite once again, and my distrust of God would become even more cemented. Here is a God whom I'm supposed to love with all my heart, mind, and soul, but He was also a God who could, and would, consistently put my love to the test by causing horrible things to happen to me.

While this story played a small part in my ever-growing unease with God, there was a story in the Bible that played a huge part in creating the chasm of trust in my heart. If you've read the whole thing, you'll know there's some messed-up stuff that happens in the Bible. But for me, this might be the most messed-up story of them all.

Father Abraham Had Many Sons

I first encountered good old Abraham early on in Sunday school. I have two distinct memories, and I'm not sure which one came first. One memory I have is learning a song called "Father Abraham," and it's kind of like the Christian "Hokey Pokey." Right foot, left foot, right arm, left arm, head in, turn around, sit down. Well it was something like that, anyway. It didn't teach me much other than this Abraham fella had a lot of kids. When I actually learned the story, though, I was a little confused. Dude only had one kid. But I was eight, so it's not as if this was pressing information. It was enough for me to get to stand up and do something sort of fun in church. Best not to screw it up by asking questions.

The other memory I have is more concrete. I'm sitting at a little oval table with a worksheet and some crayons in front of me. The picture I'm coloring is of a boy carrying a load of firewood on his back, and he's heading up a mountain. Right now, I'm coloring the wood brown. Still haven't figured out what color I'm going to make his outfit that looks like a dress.

This was a picture of Abraham's son Isaac carrying the wood up the mountain for his father, apparently unaware of the old man's intentions. Even as a kid, this story gave me pause. Let's examine it, shall we?

One day, Abraham is minding his own business when God gives him an assignment. I got off on the wrong foot with this story when it started in Genesis 22 with, "After these things God tested Abraham." Before I really understood friendship with God, the whole idea of God "testing" His friends' loyalty or love or whatever made no sense. In fact, it was a major turnoff for me ever wanting to become friends with Him. I saw how He treated the people closest to Him. No thank you. It felt like God was insecure or something, like an annoying friend who's always asking, "Are we good, man? We good?" And God asking if "we're good" looks like you having to sacrifice the thing you care about most in life. Double no thank you.

God calls out to Abraham and he answers, and God tells old Abe to take his son, Isaac, on a three-day hike to some mountain, where he's going to lay his son on an altar and light him on fire. Once he does that, God will be satisfied that Abraham loves Him.

If this weren't in the Bible and someone simply told me the story, I'd say they were trying to pervert the God I believe in by making Him look like some bloodthirsty, deranged tyrant. I'd say there's no way my God would do such a thing, because it would go against His character, which is love. I mean, if you're telling me that God would ask something of someone that even I find reprehensible as a flawed, sinful human, then I'd simply tell you that you don't know the God I serve. But the problem is that this story *is* in the Bible, and not only that, it's one of the central stories of the Old Testament. Whenever God reveals who He is to someone in the Bible, it's usually as the "God of Abraham, Isaac, and Jacob." Abraham is His man, through and through. He's the ultimate man of faith because he was willing to trust God the most. And we're all supposed to try to be like him.

One of the justifications people often use with this story is that God had no intention of ever letting Abraham go through with killing his son. So instead of some horrific test, it becomes more of a macabre practical joke designed to see what Abraham's faith is made of. But this might be even more problematic, because it gives God a sinister streak and also posits that we're all just pawns in His cosmic game.

And of course, you've got a man who isn't in on the joke and has to function for days thinking these are the last moments he will ever see his son alive. Imagine the psychological toll this must have taken on Abraham. I cannot imagine walking with my son to his death. And I can imagine even less knowing that I was going to be the one who had to kill him. If God came to me in a vacuum and asked me to do this, that would most likely be the moment that He and I parted ways for good. I say "in a vacuum" because without context and without understanding the true nature of friendship with God, this story *is* disturbing and downright appalling.

So Abraham gets his marching orders. His response? "Early the next morning" Abraham rose and started out on this task (Gen. 22:3 NIV). No hesitation, no waffling. He probably even sets an alarm so they can get an early start. I've always wondered if this was the vigor of faith or if he was just trying to leave without having to tell his wife, Sarah, what he was up to. One thing we do know: Abraham was fully committed. God had asked him to do something and he was going to do it. We know this because Scripture tells us that Abraham "considered that God was able even to raise [Isaac] from the dead" (Heb. 11:19).

What exactly makes a man walk in this level of obedience to God without even a moment's hesitation? One word: *friendship*. And there are numerous clues to the growing friendship between God and Abraham leading up to this moment.

THE CALL

Genesis 12 starts the story of Abraham (back when he was just called Abram) and there's no buildup at all, just a call from God. I've always wondered how God talked to all these people back in the Old Testament times. Did He show up in angelic form? Usually when that happened we are told so. Was it through dreams? Visions? Who knows. What we do know is that however God did it, the people He spoke to understood Him completely. All they had to do was decide whether they were going to obey or not.

It is important to note that God doesn't ask Abraham to kill his son first thing. That only comes after a world-class friendship has been built up over a fifty-year period. God will never throw you into the deep end of trust immediately, mostly because He knows we'll all drown. There is some explanation of this in the parable of the talents (Matt. 25). The Lord is aware of what natural abilities and strengths each person brings to the table, and He therefore gives a certain portion of—shall we call it favor?—to each person He chooses to work with. One might get five portions, another three, and another one. No matter what you receive from Him, it's exactly the right portion for you to handle at that moment in time.

What you do with what you've been given is the other side of things. Will you be obedient? Trustworthy? When I look back on my own journey, I realize how little I was given to start with. I've said this before, but I think it bears repeating here. I am positive I was never God's first choice to be His documentarian and to help usher in a new subgenre of faith-based films. In fact, I can prove it.

After I made my first film, *Finger of God*, I started getting emails from people all over the world, and they all pretty much said the same thing. These people were way more qualified to make films than I was (I was an English professor, for crying out loud). They told me that years ago God had put it on their hearts to make a documentary about the many miracles He was doing around the world. For whatever reason they put it off, or chickened out, or felt like they didn't have enough resources or money to do it, and now, years later, they see the movie I made as the movie *they* should have made.

It was strange to hear this over and over again, probably fifteen times in total. So I can say with confidence that at best, I was God's sixteenth choice to be His filmmaker. It's as if the Trinity sat around frustrated that all their first-round draft picks weren't panning out, so on a flyer one of them probably said, "Well, there's Wilson. He's not much to look at, but we can maybe give him a shot."

I made my first film on a twenty thousand dollar budget (spent almost entirely on travel) and borrowed camera equipment from my school. I edited everything myself in my living room. Mind you, I had never even picked up a video camera before, and I had definitely never edited anything before. I taught myself everything as I went along. The only "talent" I brought to the table was the ability to tell a story, born out of nearly fifteen years of slogging through writing project after writing project.

But I did what He asked me to do, and because of sheer obedience, He breathed on that thing, and it took off like a rocket as soon as I finished it. It looks horrible and sounds pretty horrible, but there is something about that film that even today, more than a decade later, still touches people and causes them to get excited about God again, to want more from their Christian faith than just a God-themed country club.

Then He gave me more resources and more responsibility, and even though I made a ton of mistakes along the way, my heart was always bent on obedience (even though it was reluctant obedience at first). I have found that obedience to His voice, which is simply trusting Him, the very essence of faith, is the key to true friendship with Him. Remember? "Does the LORD delight in burnt offerings and sacrifices as much as in obeying the LORD? *To obey is better than sacrifice*" (1 Sam. 15:22 NIV). And, "Without faith it is impossible to please God" (Heb. 11:6 NIV).

The Lord doesn't change, and while His first ask of Abraham would be a challenge, it wasn't so outlandish that Abraham would never be able to do it. His call to Abraham was simple and straightforward. *Move*. That's it. "Now the LORD said to Abram, 'Go from your country and your kindred and your father's house to the land that I will show you'" (Gen. 12:1).

Just move. For many of us this wouldn't be the biggest deal in the world. We move away from our families all the time. That's why we have email and FaceTime and airplanes and cell phones. Even if we move away from family and friends, we can continue in relationship with them. But this wasn't true back in the day. God was asking Abraham to break away from all the comforts of home, all the security a family clan offered, and to trust in Him alone. It wasn't an impossible ask, but it certainly wasn't an easy one.

God knew the mettle of the man He was dealing with, because in Genesis 12:4, Abraham "went, as the LORD had told him." This was God's first step toward one of the deepest friendships in history, and Abraham obeyed His voice. How many of us, though, get stuck at "move"? And usually it's not even "move from one city to another." For us, we'll get stuck and bogged down with a simple "get up off your butt and go do something I'm asking you to do."

> **God:** Go pray for that person.
> **Us:** Ooh, that's too scary. That's not my personality. I
>   don't want to look like a weirdo.
> **God:** Go call that person and tell them you forgive him
>   (or her).
> **Us:** Hmm, can't do that, Lord. Do you know how badly
>   they hurt me? Do you realize what they did to me?
>   Plus they wouldn't think they did anything wrong
>   anyway.
> **God:** Go give money to that person.
> **Us:** I can't, it's not in my budget.
> **God:** Go up to the altar; respond to the message you
>   just heard.
> **Us:** No, that's too embarrassing. People will know I
>   struggle with that if I do.

On and on it goes. God speaks to us, asks us to obey the still, small voice, and we find excuse after excuse not to obey. I have had friends I've consistently tried to reach out to in an effort to hang out more and go deeper in our friendship, but every time I do they can't get together. Something else is going on in their lives, some other event, some other excuse. And after a while I just stop calling, because it is obvious that they don't value the friendship like I do. And I don't think God is much different—at least the nature of friendship sure isn't. If He continually asks you to do things, and you continually say no, eventually He's going to move on to someone else. He'll still love you, but He'll take the favor He wanted to give you and give it to someone else He knows will listen to Him.

RIGHTEOUS BELIEF

When God makes a covenant with Abraham, the seeds of friendship are firmly planted in good soil, and there is a curious moment at the end of their conversation that deserves attention (Gen. 15). The beginning of their conversation is indicative of how God typically deals with us. Abraham is apparently minding his own business when God comes to him in a vision. We have no idea what's been going on internally with Abraham, but God seems to address something inside of him: "Fear not, Abram, I am your shield; your reward shall be very great" (Gen. 15:1).

It's fascinating that God begins by telling him everything's going to be okay, then that He's going to reward him greatly. But what is God rewarding Abraham for? The simple obedience of moving? I don't think so. I think what we're seeing here is God's heart laid open for all the world to see. He is going to reward Abraham because God is Abraham's shield. God wants to bless Abraham because God is in the blessing business. This is the true heart of the Father, not the notion that He's a despot who always wants to take something from you. The truth is, if God ever asks for something from you, it's because He is intending to give you something even better.

So God takes Abe for a walk outside and blows his hair back by telling him that he's going to have more offspring than the number of stars he sees in the sky. But Abraham and his wife are no spring chickens anymore and their childbearing days are over. God is telling Abraham that He's going to do the impossible through him, and Abraham's response is everything: "And he believed the LORD, and he counted it to him as righteousness" (Gen. 15:6).

What made Abraham righteous in God's eyes? It wasn't some mighty deed or a big check he wrote to the local charity. It was simple belief. God said something, and Abraham believed that He would do what He said. Without faith it is impossible to please God, but *with* faith we get the full attention of the Almighty.

It's also important to note that this covenant moment is steeped in experience for Abraham. God knows what is eventually coming for his friend, so He gives Abraham a number of tangible experiences to remind him that God is real. He gives Abraham a vision (Gen 15:1), then a deep sleep as well as "a dreadful and great darkness" (Gen 15:12), and finally an apparently floating, smoking fire pot and a flaming torch passing between the pieces of animals they are making covenant through. Those aren't events Abraham would soon forget!

And here's the kicker. Roughly fifteen years pass, and Abraham and Sarah still don't have the child God promised. Imagine how many days and nights they had to hear the seductive whispers of the Devil—"Did God really say?"—and lose hope in God's promise. But at no time are we given even a hint that Abraham stopped taking God at His word. And God returns fifteen years later and tells him the same thing, that He is going to give Abraham a son through Sarah and a great nation will come from him. Then, before one of the most famous events in the Bible, God finally decides to meet Abraham face-to-face.

THAT'S WHAT FRIENDS ARE FOR

As a kid, I thought the Bible was one of the most boring things to read ever. To me the Bible equalled church, and that was definitely not a place I ever looked forward to going. But there were a few tentpole stories in the Bible that caused me to sit up and take notice. One was Samson (the first action hero!) and basically the whole book of Judges (so much blood and violence!). David and Goliath was pretty cool, and Elijah's showdown with the prophets of Baal wasn't half bad either. But there was something about the destruction of Sodom and Gomorrah that especially intrigued me.

Maybe it was just that the story has an R-rated feeling to it and the payoff was explosions. But when I returned to this story as an adult pursuing a friendship with God, I saw another part of the story that I had never paid attention to before. If I had, I would have realized earlier that the point of this story isn't God's judgment. Instead, this story reveals God's heart as a friend.

Genesis 18 starts out with a bombshell, but it's played down as if it's no big deal. "And the Lord appeared to him by the oaks of Mamre, as he sat at the door of his tent in the heat of the day. He lifted up his eyes and looked, and behold, three men were standing in front of him" (Gen. 18:1–2).

Uh, okay. So the God of the universe just decided to kick it on earth with two angelic bodyguards, and along the way He decides to pop in on Abraham unannounced. I wonder if Abe was like, "Sorry about the mess, fellas, didn't know you'd be passing by." Regardless, he talks them into staying for a bit while Abraham goes all out preparing a meal like it's Thanksgiving. He then presents it to them and stands by while they eat.

And here is where my brain locks up a bit, because I am often more interested in the little, seemingly meaningless details of a Bible story than in the main narrative. Does anyone else find the picture of God, who is spirit, taking the form of a human and eating food mind-blowing? And then my mind just goes to really weird places, like does God have to go to the bathroom when He's in human form, or does the food just disappear as soon as he swallows it? Does God have to watch His carbs? Does He get garlic breath? These are the deep theological places my head often goes.

This is good news for all my fellow foodies out there. Looks like all that "heavenly feasting" talk in the New Testament isn't just metaphor. The odds are good that we're going to have an all-you-can-eat buffet for eternity available to us, and I'm assuming none of it will affect our waistlines. Like my friend and quote machine Chad Norris likes to say, "If I get to heaven and realize there's no food, I might snap."

In the middle of this impromptu dinner date, the Lord asks about Abraham's wife, Sarah. When Abraham tells God she's chilling in the tent (it's funny that God even asks where she is—He's always so accommodating to us), the Lord finally gives Abraham the big news. By this time next year, Sarah will give birth to a son. Sarah, who's eavesdropping through the tent, laughs to herself when she hears this, because she's an old lady now.

And here God shows that He's the ultimate mentalist. When Sarah laughs inwardly, God immediately asks Abraham why Sarah laughed. Sarah, knowing she's busted for eavesdropping, comes out and tries to defend herself, saying she didn't laugh. And then God simply tells her, "No, you did laugh." It's hard to tell what kind of tone God was taking, since we can only see the words. But the inclusion of this strange aside, and God making sure He gets the last word, seems to take us back to that same character trait we saw with God's interaction with Moses.

God is not a big fan of our trying to lie to Him to make ourselves look better than we are. Yet we do it all the time. We lie to Him and to ourselves about our current state; we don't fess up and take ownership of the wickedness in our hearts. I think, again, it's because we're afraid of being punished. But even when Sarah flat out lies to God, He does not bring punishment. Instead, He gently corrects her and lets her know what kind of person she's dealing with. It is also interesting to note that after God says this, Sarah shuts up. She knows she's busted.

We then get to the heart of this story and the real picture of God's heart for His friends. After everyone has eaten their fill and presumably loosened their belts, the men set out to do whatever they came here to do in the first place. Abraham, ever the gentleman, walks with them a little ways to see them off. And that's when God gives us a glimpse of His thought process in that moment.

> The LORD said, "Shall I hide from Abraham what I am about to do, seeing that Abraham shall surely become a great and mighty nation, and all the nations of the earth shall be blessed in him? For I have chosen him, that he may command his children and his household after him to keep the way of the LORD by doing righteousness and justice, so that the LORD may bring to Abraham what he has promised him." (Gen. 18:17–19)

God is about to do something to an entire city that will be talked about forever. From this day forward, the names Sodom and Gomorrah will live in infamy because of His decision. Add to that the fact that Abraham's cousin Lot lives there, and we see a picture of a God who doesn't make decisions in a vacuum of isolation, but actually looks for points of connection when He's making a big decision, as any good friend would. God is thinking to Himself as He's walking away, "I can't hide this from Abraham. I've chosen him to be my friend." God then tells Abraham what He plans on doing, even though He doesn't have to. The key to this story is that God *wants* to.

Here is another part of the story that I always misunderstood. Once Abraham knows what's going down, he has his famous "whittling down" conversation with the Lord. *What if there are fifty righteous people there, will you kill them alongside the wicked? No? Okay, what about forty-five? What about forty? Not trying to push my luck or anything, but what about thirty? Twenty?* Finally, Abraham gets, I presume, to the real number he was aiming at. *Ten.* I wonder if that's how many people were in Lot's family?

Regardless of why, the conversation makes it appear that Abraham is more merciful than God. It looks as if God was just going to nuke the whole valley, but Abraham reminds Him that there might still be good people there.

There are a couple of odd things in this story that never added up for me. First, the premise of God going to Sodom and Gomorrah makes no sense. The Lord says that He's heard a major outcry against the people in those cities, and He's going to do some recon to see if it's really as bad as everyone says it is (Gen. 18:20–21). This is just weird. Obviously God doesn't have limited knowledge of the situation—He just showed His God-ness when He read Sarah's mind and revealed her thoughts. I've heard some people suggest this is just God's way of pointing out that He's turning His full attention to the matter. But again, does God really need to take time out to fully vet a situation? I'm pretty sure, with infinite intelligence, that God gives His full attention to everything all the time.

The other part of the story that never made sense to me was that after all this, God doesn't even go down to check it out! After Abraham gets Him down to ten, verse 33 tells us, "And the LORD went His way, when He had finished speaking to Abraham." Chapter 19 begins with the two angels heading into Sodom with no God in tow. None of it made sense to me until I began to understand friendship with God.

This was never intended to be a recon mission to "find out if things are as bad as people say they are" in Sodom and Gomorrah. God already knew the full extent of the sin there, knew the hearts and minds of every person there intimately, and knew exactly what He was going to do. God being present in this scene has little to do with Sodom and Gomorrah and everything to do with Abraham. When the angels arrive in the city, the whole scene shifts from reconnaissance to a rescue mission. Their new goal is to get Lot and his family out of there before hellfire rains down.

The more I get to know the Lord, the more I realize how often He stoops to our level, often to bring us peace or to simply delight us with something. He doesn't have to tell me anything, but I have found that He enjoys telling me things—particularly things that will bring me great joy or that will cause me to fall in love with Him even more. And I think with this scene, God might have been using what He was planning to do with Sodom and Gomorrah as an excuse to hang out with Abraham for the day. Remember, God desires friendship with us, and it is obvious here that He desires friendship with Abraham.

When Jesus tells the disciples that He no longer calls them servants but instead friends, He is quick to explain what that means: "For the servant does not know what his master is doing" (John 15:15). Here, God is letting Abraham in on what He is doing, as any good friend would. He allows Abraham to bring his concerns to Him, invites conversation, listens to Abraham's heart, gives him a chance to make his case for mercy. At the end of the day, none of that conversation played any part in the ultimate judgment of Sodom and Gomorrah, because their judgment was already certain. But it *did* play a part in furthering the trust and friendship between God and Abraham. And that friendship, from day one, has been heading toward the ultimate test of a man's trust in the goodness of God.

THE FINAL EXAM

And here we go. Time to get into what for me is the hardest story in the Bible to deal with. Isaac is finally born, twenty-five years after God first promised him to Abraham (Gen. 21). *Twenty-five years.* Yet apparently Abraham never wavered in his belief in God's word.

Then, nearly fifty years after they first met, God "tests" Abraham. I could call this a lot of things, but a test wouldn't be one of them. Torture might be more appropriate. I didn't care that God was never going to let Abraham kill his son—even the idea that God would ask him to do such a thing was offensive to me. Abraham is fully convinced for three days that at the end of this hike he is going to have to kill his son.

The fact that Abraham doesn't hesitate but gets up early the next morning shows where his trust level is with God, and it also reveals the true depth of their friendship. After fifty years, there is *nothing* Abraham won't do for the Lord. And really, that's all God is asking from each and every one of us. He wants us to get to a place where we trust Him completely, where our faith is so rock solid that nothing is off limits to Him.

But even as I worked through this story with the Lord, I kept coming back to the same issue. It just didn't seem right, and it certainly didn't seem in line with "God is love." It seemed, if not mean, then certainly psychologically dubious. What exactly are you trying to get Abraham to prove to you? Don't you know the state of his heart already? Why force him through this charade in the first place?

When I was wrestling with this story for my second book, *Finding God in the Bible*, the Lord finally gave me an answer. One morning I was praying about this story, and the Lord spoke loudly and firmly. His tone startled me.

"What is your problem?" I heard Him ask me. I was taken aback.

You know what my problem is. This just doesn't seem right.

Then He hit me with the roundhouse.

"It's nothing that I didn't ask from myself, and I actually went through with it."

Check and mate. In my zeal to find justification for what God did to Abraham, I completely missed that this episode was not about finding out what Abraham was made of, but was instead a foreshadow of what God Himself would one day do to save the world. God promised Abraham a son through whom a mighty nation would arise. He then brought Abraham into a deep, trusting relationship with Him over the course of a lifetime. I don't think God's tests in our lives are ever for *Him* to find out what we're made of, but instead they are ways He shows *us* what we are made of.

The biggest tests in my life have done that. They've shown me what my faith consists of, as well as what it might be lacking. God will not tolerate idols in our hearts—anything that carries more importance to us than Him is up for the taking. I used to be terrified that God was going to ask me to give up the things I loved most because I loved those things more than I loved Him. I found my worth in them, my happiness, my joy. I was living in idolatry and calling it a career. I was worshipping idols and calling it family. But God is jealous, and if you're serious about loving and following Him, He will take a back seat to no one. And it's not because He's got an inferiority complex, but because His great desire is to have a deep friendship with you. The only way that happens is for you to clear out everything in your heart but Him.

Abraham had three days of testing, and yes, those days were awful for him. But God had to endure thirty years of walking with His Son on earth, knowing the entire time where He was leading Jesus. And this time there would be no miraculous ram in the thicket to take His place, because Jesus had to be the offering, had to be the one to conquer death, had to be crushed for our iniquities. There was no other way. If there had been, God would have found it.

And really, when it all comes down to it, the only thing God wants from us is to believe Him. To trust Him. Without faith it is impossible to please God, but with faith, it is impossible *not* to please Him.

/7/

WHAT WILL HE MAKE ME DO?

The number of times I mention my experiences with God and the Bible growing up may lead you to think I was highly traumatized by church and religious people, but that really isn't the case. My Christian upbringing was pretty normal. I attended a good, healthy church; was a regular in Sunday school and youth group; had loving parents who tried to instill godly values in me; and even attended a wonderful Lutheran school through eighth grade. I went to Christian youth camps, had a few real experiences with the Lord, and generally had a solid, godly upbringing.

Sometimes my parents read my books and scratch their heads. They don't remember church being as bad as I say it was or my constantly complaining or having angst about God and what I believed. But that's kind of the point. I was a good Christian kid, and there was an underlying sense of duty to the Christian lifestyle that didn't always invite deep, public soul searching. Keep your horrible thoughts to yourself and pretend that you think God and Christianity are as amazing as everyone else seems to think they are.

While I outwardly seemed fine with everything God-related, inwardly I was a boiling stew of questions, doubts, fears, and tangled thoughts. At thirteen, I knew I was going to be a writer, and even then I wrote stories of faith and doubt, albeit with very simple plots. But for as long as I can remember, I've had this bent inside me, a sliver of spiritual discontent. Some kids experiment with drugs or alcohol as they're trying to figure out life. That stuff never appealed to me. Ideas were always my drug of choice.

These pages contain a lifetime of pent-up frustrations, misconceptions, and inner turmoil. If I'm going to give myself over to something, I need to be 100 percent all-in. Unfortunately, the issues I had with God never allowed that to happen. I wanted Him, because people told me how amazing He was and they truly seemed happy to be in relationship with Him, but I could never quite square away the God that I was told about with the God I encountered in the Bible and in my life.

Perhaps one of my biggest misconceptions was the idea that if I gave myself fully over to the Lord, He was going to force me to do a bunch of stuff I didn't want to do. My dreams, my desires, and my passions would have to be shut away because I would now have to do "the Lord's work." And in my evangelical Christian subculture, the Lord's work was a pretty narrow window.

Once a year, my church would have what we'd call "missionary Sundays," when the missionaries we oversaw and sent funds to around the world would come in and give a short presentation to update the congregation on the kinds of things they were doing on the mission field. I thought these were better church services than most because at least I got to look at pictures instead of staring at some dude talking all morning. But they also posed a problem for my narrow view of what it meant to "leave everything for the gospel." I mean, it seemed to me that being a missionary kind of sucked.

Everything seemed difficult. It looked hot. I was pretty sure those little homes they lived in didn't have air conditioning. I was also pretty sure they didn't have cable TV, which meant no ESPN and no sports. Their food didn't look too appetizing—seemed like a lot of rice and beans. We'd often hear about how they were slowly learning the language, and I was reminded how much I hated my ninth-grade Spanish class. Then we'd see pictures of smiling faces and hear about how each one accepted Jesus, and I would immediately feel horrible about all my judgments. But that didn't make my feelings go away.

The missionaries' final statements were almost always pretty much the same: "It's definitely been tough, but it's worth it to sacrifice for the Lord. We miss some of the creature comforts of home, but we wouldn't trade our experiences with God and these people for anything." Then everyone would stand up and cheer, a special offering would be taken, and I'd put some money in to help assuage my guilt for being such a lousy Christian compared to these people.

This was the height of self-sacrifice in my Christian world, the pinnacle to which we were supposedly all striving. I mean, Jesus was pretty clear when He said, "In the same way, those of you who do not give up everything you have cannot be my disciples" (Luke 14:33 NIV). That verse, and others like it, absolutely terrified me. Deep down, my biggest fear was that God was somehow going to make me become a missionary and move to

Africa. I'm pretty sure that's every evangelical kid's worst night-mare at some point in their life.

If I had a love-hate relationship with the Father and I completely ignored the Holy Spirit, then it's safe to say I had an uneasy truce with Jesus. I couldn't deny that He loved me. That truth was rock solid. You don't die for someone you don't love. But I also couldn't get past how often in the Gospels He came across as intense and inflexible. Sure, He'd say things like, "My yoke is easy and my burden is light" (Matt. 11:30 NIV). But then He'd turn right around and say something like, "If anyone comes to me and does not hate his own father and mother and wife and children and brothers and sisters, yes, and even his own life, he cannot be my disciple" (Luke 14:26). Okay, so which one is it? Because you say your yoke is easy and your burden is light, but asking me to give up everything, even my own family, sure doesn't seem easy and light!

Even when someone would come across Jesus' path who was really trying hard to do the right thing, it seemed like Jesus would find one more thing, that pressure point, that would really hurt. It felt like no one could ever measure up to His impossibly high standards.

Take the story of the rich young ruler, for example. Jesus is on his three-year kingdom world tour, selling out fields and mead-ows everywhere, when a young man approaches and humbly kneels before Him. The kid asks Jesus what he needs to do to obtain eternal life, and Jesus gives him the company answer. *You know the commandments. Do those.* The young man then tells Him that he's kept all the commandments since he was a child. So Jesus ratchets it up a notch and tells him the last thing he needs to do is sell everything he has and give to the poor, then come and follow Him. This bums the kid out because he's super wealthy, and he walks away dejected.

I get the point of this story is to show that our riches are in heaven, not here on earth, and that we can have no other gods before Him. But I was always more interested in the humanity of this story than the moral of it. It seems this kid is sincere. He's humble, inquisitive, and really wants to do well in God's eyes. But instead of encouragement, he gets a sucker punch.

But there is a telling statement in this story that is easy to miss. I always saw Jesus in this story as being impossible to please and overly demanding. But jammed right in the middle of all this is a blink-and-you'll-miss-it moment that should change the narrative a bit: "And he said to Him, 'Teacher, I have kept all these things from my youth up.' Looking at him, *Jesus felt a love for him* and said to him, 'One thing you lack . . .'" (Mark 10:20–21 NASB).

What an important detail. Without it, this can easily be read as Jesus trying to find a pressure point to teach a lesson about wealth. But with it, Jesus is exactly who He says He is. Jesus saw something in this young man's heart that was genuine, something that had the fragrance of love for others and for God, and in return He felt a love for the young man swell inside of Him. Love always responds to love.

I used to read this story and see what I wanted to see. A rejection. *Sorry kid, you're not good enough because you don't want to sell everything you have and become a missionary.* I saw a God who wanted to force this young man to do something he didn't want to do to prove his love for Him. But this was no rejection; this was an invitation. Jesus offered this "rich young ruler" a seat at His table as a part of His inner circle of friends. His name could have been talked about for thousands of years, and stories and sermons and devotions could have been written using the many adventures and lessons he learned in his friendship with Jesus—with God Himself. This was an extraordinary offer.

Jesus doesn't look for pressure points; He simply looks into our hearts. He is not trying to find something to pick apart, and He's not trying to find that one thing you're most terrified of doing because He wants to test your feelings for Him. He's just looking to see if there is anything in your life that is an idol—something that you deem more important than God.

While filming my movies around the world, I've seen lots of man-made gods and idols. I've been in small homes with tiny shrines to demons in a corner, and I've walked through massive temples filled with statues and smoke and noise and people desperately trying to make their magic gods happy so they can get something from them. In settings like that, it's easy to identify idolatry.

But then I come home and I walk around a shopping district or go to a sporting event or even glance around my own home at my entertainment options and my full refrigerator and the picture of all my kids or my beloved dogs and suddenly it becomes much more difficult to identify my own idolatry. We don't have asher poles we worship in America, but we do have field goal posts in stadiums. We do have "mothers, fathers, husband, wives, children" in our lives whom we consider more important than anything God would ask of us. The idol may change, but the idolatry stays the same.

I've gone through seasons in which I've lost or nearly lost people, dreams, a company, a dog, or whatever else meant the world to me, and each time God brings me to a place where I have a decision to make. Either I can hold onto this thing that has become an idol in my heart, that I feel like I can't live without, that I spend way more time obsessing over than I do the Lord, or I can choose to place it on the altar of my heart and offer it up to God. What He does with it is up to Him. He may take it (which He's done) or He may take it and replace it with something even better (which He's also done), but I have learned time and time again that anything in my life that keeps me from an undiluted friendship with Him is something to be hated. Nothing is worth giving up a friendship with the God of the universe. With my Father. My Jesus. My Spirit. They are my dearest friends, and my life depends on them.

So when Jesus tells this rich young ruler to do one more thing, He is simply asking him to make a decision. Do you love money or Me most? And when the man walks away from Him, Jesus doesn't rain down judgment on him, but instead simply states the obvious. It's tough for someone to have the kind of hunger you need to become true friends with God when that person doesn't feel the need for God because they're comfortable. And instead of becoming one of the great people of faith in the Bible, we never even learn the kid's name.

Get in My Belly!

One of the most famous stories in the Bible about God asking someone to do something they don't want to do is the story of Jonah. This story was a staple in my Sunday school years because it had everything you need to keep a kid's attention. It also had a neat little lesson built in, namely, that you can never run from God. Again, definitely a true point to note, but to this kid's mind that wasn't something to be celebrated. It just made God into an unstoppable force who could haunt me whenever He wanted. But the story, as I read it now as a friend of God, is a little different than they taught me on felt boards and in vegetable cartoons.

Jonah was God's prophet, which back in the day was a big deal. The Lord dealt with the prophets directly, so they were His main delegates to give people messages. One day God speaks to Jonah and tells him to book a trip to the great city of Nineveh because the people there have been super naughty. God wants Jonah to go warn the city that they must repent of their evil ways or else God is going to bring about their destruction.

As we learn later in the story, God's showing mercy to enemies of Israel is beyond scandalous to Jonah, and he, through a misguided attempt to save God from Himself, books the first boat out that is going in the opposite direction of Nineveh. He wants no part of this plan of God's to help his enemies, because Jonah is a true patriot of Israel. But God isn't interested in Jonah's patriotism; He's interested in his obedience.

You probably know how the rest of the story goes, so I'll keep it brief. Jonah hitches a ride on a boat in his effort to run away from God's assignment, and God is like, *Uh, not so fast.* He sends a massive storm that threatens to sink the ship, and the men on board are understandably freaked out. They believe the storm is happening because someone on board has done something wrong, so they cast lots to see who the guilty one is. Of course it falls on Jonah. He explains that he's running away from God and tells them the only way this can stop is if they hurl him overboard.

The men aren't too keen on this idea because they'd be murdering someone, but the storm gets worse and worse until they're at the point of desperation. Probably figuring they're all going to die anyway, they grab Jonah and heave him overboard, and immediately the storm calms. This so shakes the pagan sailors that they offer a sacrifice to Yahweh and make vows to serve Him!

That's when Jonah goes all Pinocchio and gets swallowed up by a massive fish. Because of Disney movies I had the mental image of Jonah hanging out in a cavernous belly surrounded by driftwood and seaweed. But the truth would have been much, much worse. Claustrophobic, fleshy, gag-inducing smelly, and probably constantly deprived of oxygen, the fact that he survived for three days is a miracle in itself. It's like the most intense time-out ever recorded in human history.

After Jonah is sufficiently humbled, he prays to the Lord and is finally vomited out of the fish onto dry land. Ugh, that's like the ultimate degradation—puked out of a fish. Nasty.

Sometimes Scripture cracks me up with its understated humor. The verse after Jonah is released from the fish says, "Then the word of the LORD came to Jonah the second time, saying, 'Arise, go to Nineveh'" (Jonah 3:1–2). It's such a boss parent thing to do. After Jonah's time-out is over, God calmly says the same thing He said to Jonah at the beginning. And this time Jonah obeys. Smart lad.

And what do you know, when Jonah gets to Nineveh and warns them of God's coming judgment, the entire city, including their leadership, repents and turns from their evil. But then there's a little twist ending, and we need to examine the roles and hearts of each person in the story to reach the real point.

Far from being overjoyed that his ministry was fruitful and he just participated in helping to save an entire city, Jonah is furious. He goes on a massive pout fest. He yells at God for His mercy, and basically flops down on the ground like a bratty teenager and tells God to just kill him now because this whole thing is just *so* horrible. At this point, if I'm God, I'm taking this guy to the woodshed. But of course, God is merciful, even when we act like jerks, and He causes a plant to grow overnight to give shade to Jonah, who has taken a seat outside the city in hopes that God will see reason and destroy the city. The next day, the plant withers and dies, and Jonah is about to get heat stroke. So once again he throws a temper tantrum and tells God to just go ahead and kill him already.

God tries to reason with Jonah, telling him he's crying over losing a plant he didn't even labor over, so why wouldn't God have concern over a massive city of people who simply didn't know any better? The book then ends abruptly, and we never learn if Jonah finally got his head straight. My guess, judging by his actions throughout the story, is that no, Jonah never did.

A few points in this story show us God's wonderful nature and help us chop down my earlier view that Jonah's story shows a God who forces you to do things you don't want to do and pushes you around to get His way. The first thing to note is that none of this should have happened. Yes, God is asking Jonah to do something he doesn't want to do, but what is God's motivation and what is Jonah's? The image of God as a tyrant is broken by the fact that He simply wants to give His kids a chance to repent and choose Him. Jonah considers the people of Nineveh to be enemies of Israel, therefore enemies of God, and he wants judgment, not mercy. The truth is, God is who He always says He is in this story: love. Jonah is—well, there's no other way to put it—he's a religious jerk.

I've often wondered why God goes to all these lengths to

get Jonah to do what He's asking. When Jonah runs from his assignment, why doesn't God just find another prophet to go to Nineveh? Was God trying to teach Jonah a lesson? It's possible, but there may be another explanation. Maybe God has specific assignments for people because those people can accomplish the tasks in a way others can't. We always think God can pick and choose any random person to do His bidding, but that may not be the case. Maybe another reason God is so adamant about obedience from us is that He really *does* know everything, and when we say no to Him, we are basically saying no to His mission of love for the world around us. For whatever reason, God wanted Jonah to be the man to give His message to Nineveh, and Jonah saying no meant a lot of people were going to die in their sin.

Notice another important piece of this story: God loves Jonah. I'm immediately turned off by Jonah's worldview and his seeming manic desire to see people punished. He is not a man of mercy but a man of judgment. Jonah acts like a spoiled brat, and even when he sits down outside the city hoping God will bring judgment on the city, God has mercy on him and provides him with shade. You can see God's gentleness with Jonah in their final conversation, like a patient Father trying to teach a life lesson to His son. When I think back to all the lies I used to believe about God's character, particularly when it came to my own bad behavior, here is a story that clearly shows how God approaches us.

I used to see this story as one that showed my own powerlessness against God, because He'll make my life miserable until He gets what He wants. But Jonah's heart should be on trial here, not God's. God shows nothing but mercy for both Jonah and a pagan city. God's dealing with a punk who has no love in his heart, but He needs that punk to reveal the love in His heart for an entire city. *So yeah, Jonah, you're going to get your behind on a boat and do what I'm asking of you, which is literally your job title, because I want my kids back.*

This is similar to an aspect of Christianity today that saddens me, and it's one I am constantly fighting against. I call them "angry, mean Christians," and they are so similar to Jonah it's uncanny. These are the Christians who preach hellfire and brimstone and judgment, and they get angry with the message of God's love and mercy. They're the ones who tell me that I'm lying to people because I'm not telling them that they're going to burn in hell if they don't repent. While it is true that Jonah went to tell the people of Nineveh to repent, it was the loving heart of God for the people that drove the message. This was also before Jesus' time. Now that Jesus has conquered sin and death, we can introduce people to Jesus and let the Holy Spirit do the convicting. He's a lot better at it than we are, that's for sure.

These angry, mean Christians say they want repentance, but it has to come the way they say it should. If someone finds God through His kindness and not the fear of judgment, they accuse people of preaching a "different" Jesus and "tickling the ears." But the kindness of God is *the* thing that leads people to repentance (Rom. 2:4). So while the judgment-heavy Christians think they're protecting some pure strain of Christianity, in reality they are the ones preaching a different Jesus and tickling their own ears. They call themselves Christians, they know the lingo, and maybe they really are believers. But like Jonah, sometimes they can be real religious jerks.

OBEDIENCE VERSUS DESIRE

When God puts something on your heart or He makes clear what His desire is for your life, and it's something you don't want to do, how do you react? I've seen people react in all kinds of ways, but one of the most destructive reactions I've seen is the idea that somehow God cares more about your "heart" (desire) than your obedience. This is flat-out not true. Throughout Scripture, God is constantly asking people to do things they don't want to do, and those people respond in a wide variety of ways, just like the rest of us. Some obey immediately, others take a while, and others stomp off in rebellion and must face the consequences of choosing a life outside of what God intended.

What are we so afraid of, anyway? Why do we resist what He asks of us? I think it's because even though we can only see a small part of the picture, we *think* we can see it all. That, or we make a decision based on our limited view of things because that's all we can understand and all that we are capable of doing at this moment. But God has shown time and time again that if He is asking something of us, He will give us whatever is needed to follow through, and He may very well bring a greater blessing to you than you ever thought possible.

Perhaps nowhere is this truth made more evident than with Jesus Himself as He prays on the Mount of Olives before His crucifixion. Jesus knows what is coming, knows what God is asking Him to do, and He even knows why He has to do it. But Jesus doesn't *want* to do it. He prays, "Father, if you are willing, remove this cup from me" (Luke 22:42).

The next time you think God would never ask you to do something you don't want to do, just look at Jesus in that garden.

No one has ever been loved by the Father like Jesus has, but even He had to make a choice to submit and walk out something He desperately didn't want to do. We say God cares about our hearts above all else, but what we do reveals our hearts. Jesus obeyed the Father because He loved and trusted the Father.

I used to live in constant fear that God would ask me to do something I didn't want to do, and for once, my fears were grounded in truth. God asks me to do stuff all the time that I don't want to do! But every time I walk in obedience, two things happen: He gets me through it; and I come out the other side a better man, a better son, and a better friend of God.

/8/

GOD'S LOVE IS LIKE THE LOTTERY

I travel a lot, and every once in a while as I'm moving through an airport or walking in a large city and am surrounded by a gaggle of people, I have the same thought. *Most of the people I'm looking at probably don't know Jesus, and here they are just rolling through life, trying to pay their mortgages, keep their jobs, get to the weekend, or whatever. How in the world is Jesus going to win all these hearts when there is so much in the world working against Him?* It's an overwhelming feeling I get and I don't like it, so I usually just put on some headphones to drown out the heaviness with some tunes.

But something else, something even more troublesome, has been made plain to me as I've traveled to more than forty countries around the world. The reality is that the vast majority of people alive today are struggling. Poverty is staggering, living situations are beyond rough, and the evil present in the world is enough to make you want to curl up in a ball of helplessness.

A highlight in many of my films is when I hear the Lord telling me to travel to the other side of the world, and I then have to go in faith and figure out why God wanted me to go there to film. Here's an example of what it's like.

When it was time to make my fourth film, *Holy Ghost*, I wanted to do things differently than I did with my first three films. In those movies I would go somewhere to film either an established ministry or a missionary in a certain part of the world. If nothing happened when we went out on the streets to film, at least I'd have what was going on with the ministry to fall back on. Such was my enormous and unshakable faith back then. But after three movies and six years of growing in friendship with God, by the time I got to *Holy Ghost* I was ready to take a true step of faith. I wanted to attempt to make the first film in history that was, as much as is humanly possible, completely led and directed by the Holy Spirit. Who better to lead a film about the Holy Spirit than the Holy Spirit Himself?

But how exactly do you do something like that? For me, it mostly meant praying a lot and then shutting up to listen to what God was saying. I had grown a ton in hearing the Lord's voice over the years, but I was no Moses, that's for sure. But God was gracious, and I think He really likes it when we step out in radical faith, so He would speak to me in visions during my prayer times or give me or others dreams, and together these little clues began to take enough shape that I could start booking trips with my crew.

An example of how this worked was our trip to Monaco. Months before, I was in my Chicago studio having morning devotions when I got a strong impression to begin praying about the trip we had planned for Italy and Greece. The Lord had already shown me a few places He wanted me to film, but I still had two days that were open, so I was waiting for Him to tell me where to go. When I got the impression, I knew the Lord was about to tell me where to go for those two days.

Many people don't understand how things work between me and God for these films, and I've found that many think it is like some mystical trance where I'm transported to the third heaven amid dancing unicorns and rainbows, but the reality is far more mundane. I'm human and fallible, and hearing God is as much about learning what His heart is for a situation as it is hearing direct coordinates. I've found that often He will be vague, because this is a friendship and a partnership after all, and I think He delights in giving me some leeway to go places I would like to see.

While this may spark some debate for those who think God isn't interested in our ideas, keep in mind that after God made all the animals, He called Adam over to name them. God did this "to see what he would call them" (Gen. 2:19). Adam naming the animals God had just created is about as co-laboring, partnership stuff as you can get.

So going into this time of prayer, and sensing what was coming, my mind immediately went into producer mode as I ran ahead of God to try and guess where we'd be going. I told you, I'm human. But as I heard the Lord tell me to pull up a map of the Italy and Greece region, I wondered if He might send me to some biblical spot like Patmos. That would be pretty cool.

But when I looked at the map and Patmos in particular—I don't know how else to explain this—it looked "cold." I was just looking at a name on a screen. Huh. Okay, so not there, I guess. I started looking around the map at random, wondering if I was doing this wrong, when I saw it. *Monaco.* It was "hot," and I just stared. I knew nothing about Monaco other than it was a place rich people went, and I think it was in *Iron Man 2.* I also couldn't figure out why God would want to send me there. Could I even afford to go there?

So I just prayed, "God, do you want me to go film in Monaco?" I can't say I heard an audible voice booming from heaven saying, "Yes, my son." But I did get a fleeting image of a brown boat, and I got the sense that we needed to get on that boat for some reason. And that's it. So I told my team what had just happened, then immediately started making plans to spend two days in Monaco during our time in Italy and Greece.

Turns out Monaco *is* expensive (thirteen dollars for a Coke?), so my measly film budget could only allow us to stay one night there. But I dragged my crew and my friend Todd White with me, and we had one day to figure out why God sent us there. All we had to go on was a hazy picture of a brown boat I had received three months before.

Did I mention the place was expensive? I quickly realized that feeding my crew was going to be problematic on my budget, so I found the one place in the city where we could get a meal that wouldn't take gold bullion to pay for it. A pizza joint. We had lunch there and immediately set about talking to the locals with the one piece of information we had. Does anyone know where we can find someone with a boat?

A nice couple overheard us and told us that we should head down to the harbor (duh, boats) and look for a place called Stars and Bars, and there might be someone there who could help us. I have no idea why this couple thought someone at a random restaurant could help us, but hey, it was our first and only lead, so we went with it. After eating we grabbed our stuff and walked down to the harbor. When we got there, Todd struck up a conversation with a lady and she wound up having a beautiful encounter with the Lord. This was great, and it happened in *front* of a boat, so maybe that was why we were here?

Then something happened that had never happened to me while shooting for more than a decade. It started to rain. In more than ten years of filming, I had never lost a day of shooting because of rain. It might rain on the day we arrived or left, or rain when we were planning on filming indoors, but it had *never* rained on a day we were planning on shooting outside. And here we were, our only day to film in Monaco, which, *might I remind You, Lord, is where You sent me to film, and You're going to let it rain us out?* We dashed for cover, trying to protect our equipment, and ended up sitting at some tables outside a restaurant while the heavens opened up in a way that would have made Noah sit up and take notice.

While we sat there, Todd ordered an orange juice and I sulked. These are the times when making these movies is beyond stressful for me. The crew is just doing their thing; they don't really care that it's raining because they're getting paid whether we film or not. But this whole thing was riding on my shoulders, more specifically if I had heard God correctly or not, and right then it was looking very much like what I had experienced in my studio three months earlier was nothing more than a reaction to the burrito I had eaten the night before. Even if we did find someone with a boat, it wasn't as if we could take it out in the storm. I was confused and upset. The weather was always my thing, man. *God, I thought we had an understanding here.*

While we were sitting there, two women walked by us. One needed to use a cane to function. When Todd sees someone limping, it's like a shark smelling blood in the water. He sprang up out of his seat and approached the two women, asking if he could pray for the lady who was limping. The crew and I stayed in our seats, quietly filming this encounter, and I slid on my headphones to hear the conversation. After praying for the women, Todd told them we were making a film about the Holy Spirit and we were trying to find someone with a boat. One of the women asked why we needed a boat, and he said we weren't sure, but maybe we could film an interview on it or something. The woman then said that she might know someone with a boat we could use, and could we come back in like three hours? Of course we could. Just come back here? Yes. Where's here?

That's when I finally looked up and saw it. We were sitting right outside Stars and Bars. Oh, and the lady who was going to see if she could help us? She was the owner of the place.

It's times like that, when you're in the "pre-miracle" space, as I like to call it, and you know God is about to come through and all you have to do is walk forward and open your gift, when you realize yet again how amazing God is. While I sulk and complain, God is busy doing His thing for me. I'm yelling at Him for making it rain on us, but He actually *made* it rain so it would force us to scramble over to the very place we needed to be, at the very moment we needed to be there. And of course, not twenty minutes after we had that encounter, the storm stopped and the blue skies returned. God is amazing at what He does, in case you weren't aware.

We had some time to kill, so we walked around looking at

all the amazing yachts, and at one point Todd saw the prince of Monaco's palace on the top of the mountain overlooking the harbor. He pointed at it and said, "Dude, I want to go up there! We should see if God could get us in there!" I turned to him and said, "Todd, that's where the prince lives, man, that would be impossible to do in the time we have here. Let's just stay focused on finding this boat." He reluctantly agreed but made it clear how cool it would be if we could film in the palace. It was definitely not my finest hour of faith, and God would teach me an important lesson before the day was out.

When we finally made it back to Stars and Bars three hours later, our new friend was waiting for us. Come to find out, we were going to *her* boat, but it wasn't in the main harbor, so we had to walk a little ways. When we finally reached it, I turned the corner and stopped dead in my tracks.

It was a brown boat.

Once we were on board, she showed us around and we were finally able to tell her the story behind why we were there. It became obvious to everyone, even her, that God's hand was on the meeting, and after we did our interview with Todd on the boat (which she listened to, hearing over and over about the love of God), she invited us to dinner at her restaurant. Before we left the boat, though, Todd jokingly asked her if she'd ever met the prince of Monaco.

"Yes."

"Have you ever talked to him?"

"Yes."

We all went quiet.

"Do you . . . like . . . know him?"

"Yes, we actually grew up together. Not only that, but we're in his personal boat slip right now. He doesn't need a boat, so he lets me use it."

I was floored. *You have got to be kidding me.* I immediately repented to the Lord—*I will never doubt You again.* And then Todd just went for it.

"Is there any chance we can go to the palace to meet him?"

"Oh my gosh guys, he would love to meet you all, but he's in Russia at the moment and won't be back for a few more days."

Lesson complete. You would think someone who has seen as much impossible stuff as I have would never doubt God's ability to make something happen, but believing in the impossible isn't easy! Had the prince been in town, we would have been on our way to meet him, just like Todd had asked for. Truly nothing is impossible for God.

We went to dinner with her and everything came together—it finally made sense why the Lord had shown me a boat in Monaco three months before. It was all designed to get us to that moment. Our friend was a believer who had lost touch with the Lord, and as the love of the Father washed over her that night, she reconnected to a God who loved her so extravagantly that He sent a film crew of perfect strangers to her doorstep through a series of whispers, visions, chance encounters, and a rainstorm. It was a powerful picture of how far God would go to pursue the one sheep that had strayed from Him.

In the film this whole scene is shown as it happens, and it's great. But even as I have filmed this and countless other encounters just like it, I am left with a slew of new questions to wrestle with. The biggest is this: There were thousands of people who needed a touch from God that day in Monaco. So why did our friend get chosen over everyone else? Did she just happen to win the God lottery that day?

Some may look at a question like that as silly. After all, who cares? God blessed someone and we should be celebrating it. And I get that, and I do celebrate it. It's why I continue to film God doing it! But things get a little trickier when we move from blessing to tragedy.

RANDOM ACTS OF GODNESS

The reality of this dilemma hit home while I was filming one of my television shows, *Questions with God*. In the show, I gather various friends of mine, many of whom I've filmed with over the years, for a series of roundtable discussions where we wrestle with the very kinds of questions I'm bringing up in this book. During one of the episodes about whether or not God is the cause of your problems, a good friend of mine who is a pastor in Florida, Darren Davis, told us about two stories that had recently happened to him.

Two people who attended his church had been involved in major car accidents that week. Both were beautiful people and lovers of Jesus, but each had a different outcome. One car accident was horrific and shouldn't have left any survivors, but the girl came out with barely a scratch. The other accident was minor in comparison, but the girl had died. So on the one hand, Darren told us, we come together as a body to celebrate God's protection over the one, but we also have to attend the funeral of the other.

There are other examples. I filmed a man in Russia named Victor who used to be the head of communist indoctrination for youth over all of Siberia. My friend Robby Dawkins, who has filmed with me more than almost anyone, was in Russia speaking at some churches when his host took him to a local bar for some food. While they were sitting there, Victor walked in and the host pointed him out to Robby and told him who he was. He asked Robby if he'd like to meet Victor, and Robby said sure, why not.

They walked up to Victor and the host blurted out, "Hey, Victor, I want to introduce you to Robby Dawkins. He's a prophet from America and he's about to tell you things about your life that no one else knows." He then looked at Robby and said, "Have a go at him, Robby."

Of course, Robby was pretty shocked by this quick turn of events, but he was in the middle of it now, so he figured he might as well see if God gave him anything. He prayed internally, then opened his mouth, having no idea what he was going to say. What came out was, "I see smoke, water, and fire. Three times in your life you almost died, and all three times something or someone saved you, and you have no idea who it was. But Jesus wants you to know that it was Him who saved you, and He's inviting you into a relationship with Him right now."

Okay, that was pretty specific, and even Robby was surprised by it. He had no idea if it was true, but that's what the Holy Spirit said through him.

Victor stared at him, then looked at the host. He looked back at Robby and said, "How do you know these things?" He then told Robby about three events where he almost died, the most harrowing happening on a submarine while he was in the navy. The reason no one knew about that event was because they had been on a secret mission and were in waters they were not allowed to be in, and something had gone wrong with the submarine. Smoke had filled the sub, and men were scrambling to get out. In the confusion, Victor got turned around and couldn't find the exit. The smoke was so thick he couldn't see his hand in front of his face. He collapsed, knowing he was about to die, when strong hands grabbed him, pulled him up the stairs, and flung him outside the sub. He looked around to see who had saved him, but no one was there.

He looked hard at Robby and told him no one had ever heard that story because they were sworn to secrecy on account of the illegality of their mission. Even his wife didn't know this had happened to him. Robby smiled and told him again that Jesus was the one who had saved him, that Jesus had been pursuing him his whole life, and that He wanted a relationship with him. Victor wound up becoming a Christian that night and is still an active member in his church in Siberia.

I remember being at a church youth camp when I was a teenager. A girl was there with her leg in a cast and one heck of a story to tell. She had been out on a boat with some family and friends when the boat took a sharp turn and she fell overboard. Her leg hit the propeller and was cut deeply, and she became entangled in some ropes that were hanging into the water. She couldn't move, and she knew she was about to drown. In desperation she used her last breath to scream out the name of Jesus, and she said when she did, it was as if her voice echoed through the water. Instantly, strong hands grabbed hold of her, untied the ropes from around her, then pushed her to the surface. When she emerged, no one was in the water with her, and everyone was looking over the other side of the boat. Jesus had saved her life.

These stories amaze me, and they reiterate how great, loving, and powerful Jesus is. But for every story we hear of God's amazing protection or deliverance, there are countless others where the soldier dies at sea or the child drowns in the lake. One person is miraculously spared in a car crash, and the other dies. For many, especially those who must suffer through the tragedy where God didn't provide a miracle, there will forever be a gaping hole in their souls—one that was created by a simple question for which there is no answer. *Why?*

In Luke 13, Jesus deals with this. Some people ask Him about a tragedy that had happened where Pilate apparently killed some Galileans in the Jewish temple. Jesus asks, "Do you think that these Galileans were worse sinners than other Galileans, because they suffered in this way?" His answer is no. He then brings up another recent tragedy: "Or those eighteen on whom the tower in Siloam fell and killed them: do you think that they were worse offenders than all the others who lived in Jerusalem? No, I tell you; but unless you repent, you will all likewise perish" (Luke 13:2–5).

Jesus is clear: Accidents happen, and bad people do bad things. A tragedy is not divine judgment on an individual. He also doesn't linger on the question very long, because to God, the long view is the only view worth anything. We are obsessed with the short view—with what we are going through *right now*. We have an entire book of psalms that deals with David's struggle with the short view of his life. *Where are You, God? When are You going to show up for me? How much longer are You going to remain silent while my enemies gear up to destroy me? Are You even there? Do You even care?*

And when we hear stories of miraculous escapes of others, but not for us or for our loved ones, we start to wonder what's wrong with us. Did we do something wrong, or is God punishing us for something?

THE FORGOTTEN ELEMENT

It's time to head into some tricky theological weeds, and I'm barely going to touch the surface, but I want to point out a few things we often forget when dealing with bad things happening to good people. We have been deeply ingrained with the idea that God is basically controlling everything, which is why we tend to blame Him for everything bad that happens. But while God is certainly *over* everything, there is a sticky fly in the ointment called free will that complicates things exponentially.

As we all know, love is risky. In romance, there comes that point when you're full to bursting with feelings and you realize you are going to have to tell that certain someone how you feel about them. It's a terrifying moment for most people because you don't know what they're going to say. There is real risk involved, a risk of having your heart broken. Love, to be truly love, must be chosen in complete freedom. If you are coerced, pressured, forced, or guilted into loving someone, then it isn't actually love. Only in total freedom can true love be chosen or given. This is a core principle of love.

This is why God chose to give us free will in the first place: for love. He could have done any number of things in creating us that would have bent us toward choosing Him, but He understood that only by giving us *total* freedom to choose or reject Him could our love be genuine. But by doing so, He subjected Himself to a level of rejection by His creation the scale of which is impossible to fathom. And before you think it doesn't affect Him, just read a little of the Old Testament and you will start to get a feel for how much the rejection of His people bothers Him. His "jealousy" comes from a place of deep love and affection for us. The picture of a bride and bridegroom permeates the Scriptures for a reason.

This free will, remember, is also why He must remain invisible. If He reveals Himself in fullness, our free will is basically toast because we will be overpowered by His glory. Essentially, He must hide Himself in a sense to keep an even playing field.

We typically only view free will through the lens of choosing or rejecting Jesus, but it is actually the foundation on which all creation is built. We are free to choose whatever selfless or selfish choice we want. Demons and angels are free to choose their actions. To think that simply because we have a relationship with God therefore means that God is bound to intervene on our behalf to constantly make sure nothing bad ever happens to us is to miss the point of relationship entirely.

We think the world revolves around us because, in truth, our world *does* revolve around us. Our thoughts are consumed with our own lives, our own decisions, our own problems, and our own desires. We care about the people who exist within our personal orbit. If something bad happens to someone we don't know it is a "senseless tragedy." If that same bad thing happens to us or someone we are close to, it often turns into a major spiritual crisis and will in many ways mark us forever. This is basic human nature.

But it isn't God's nature. He is deeply invested in all His children. Some who have opened their hearts to Him have the benefit of "hiding beneath the shade of His wings," of holding to the rock of salvation, and having the favor of God upon them. Those who have rejected Him don't have that covering, but they do exist in a world where God will pursue them until the day they die. When we continue to make poor decisions that reject Him, often He will withdraw and simply let us have what we want—much to our own detriment. And then we have the audacity to wonder why God would allow bad consequences for our bad decisions!

It would be one thing if we only had to worry about our own decisions within our tiny, limited world. But what happens when other decisions from other "worlds" begin to crash into ours? And then other decisions, and other decisions beyond those, all continue to crash into one another, leaving behind destruction, heartache, and consequences. A man making a choice that he no longer wants to be with his wife results in very real, very painful consequences for that wife, their children, and their friends. We want to turn people's poor choices into indictments against God, but really, they're just poor choices made out of our own brokenness, fear, and sinful natures.

One of the most misunderstood verses in the Bible is Romans 8:28: "And we know that for those who love God all things work together for good, for those who are called according to his purpose." A person makes a terrible decision in their free will, which in turn causes a tragic outcome, and because God is amazing, He works with what He's been given to turn as much of that tragic outcome as possible into something good. But by doing so, He creates an outcome that appears to have been orchestrated by Him from the beginning.

Let's say a guy gets drunk and drives a car. As a result of this poor decision, he hits and kills a child walking home from school. The family of the child is devastated, wondering why God allowed such a thing to happen, but their faith in God pushes through and at the funeral they publicly forgive the man who killed their child. A family member who never believed in God is present and is so overcome by this act of forgiveness that his heart is opened to God's grace in his own life and he chooses to accept Jesus.

Now the real question is: Did God kill this family's child in order for this other person to be saved? Many would say yes because they think God is pulling all the strings. But with free will in play, God *can't* be pulling all the strings, because then free will wouldn't exist. God went to work with the carnage in front of Him based on one man's horrible choice, and He "worked it together for good." But to a casual observer, it certainly appears that this was God's plan all along. It wasn't. His plan was for this young child to grow up to become a beautiful person and live a long life, but the free choice of another person smashed into the world of the child and changed everything.

Our lives may seem fairly simple to us, but the universe we live in is infinitely complicated. As much as I'd love to accept the "our choices affect others and God just has to deal" argument, I also realize there is one more part to all this that complicates things so much that I ultimately have to throw up my hands and accept that I really don't know much of anything. Sometimes God *does* involve Himself in our lives to stop something horrible from happening. And if He does that for some but not everyone, we're right back where we started.

My dad told me a story that he could never explain logically. When he was a kid, he was running in his neighborhood, playing a game, and he dashed into the street. Instantly, he found himself running in the opposite direction, leaving the street and back on the sidewalk. He stopped running, more than confused by what had just happened, and at that instant a school bus barreled down the street behind him. Had God not miraculously turned him around, he would have been dead before the age of ten. He would never have grown up, gotten married, had my sister and me, and we would never have had our respective kids. I never would have made the movies that have touched so many, and you wouldn't be reading this book right now.

So why was my dad saved from the bus and another child isn't? Short answer: I have no idea. And neither does anyone else. This is where faith gets its potency, because faith with no opposition isn't really faith at all. It's just a belief or an observation. We think believing that Jesus is real, died on a cross, and rose from the dead is the be-all and end-all of faith, when even the demons believe those things to be true! But true faith is what you do when nothing makes sense anymore. That's the faith that moves mountains, that brings peace that passes all understanding, and that causes even Jesus to pause and marvel.

THE ONE GUY WHO IMPRESSED JESUS

Jesus has just entered Capernaum when He's approached by a centurion asking for His help. He has a servant at home who is paralyzed and suffering greatly. Jesus doesn't hesitate and tells the man He'll go with him to heal his servant. But then the centurion does something that stops Jesus in His tracks.

> But the centurion replied, "Lord, I am not worthy to have you
> come under my roof, but only say the word, and my servant

CHASING A GOD YOU DON'T WANT TO CATCH

will be healed. For I too am a man under authority, with soldiers under me. And I say to one, 'Go,' and he goes, and to another, 'Come,' and he comes, and to my servant, 'Do this,' and he does it." When Jesus heard this, *he marveled* and said to those who followed him, "Truly, I tell you, with no one in Israel have I found such faith." (Matt. 8:8–10)

What was it that caused the God of the universe to stop in His tracks and marvel at someone? Obviously it was this man's faith, but what made his faith different from others? After all, there are plenty of other examples in the Gospels of people exerting faith that Jesus could heal them or someone they love. I think the centurion's faith was so staggering to Jesus because of how overt and commanding it was. Jesus has already offered to heal the man and has probably even started moving to go. But the centurion stops Him. He is a man who understands the authority of Christ—*no need for you to show up personally, Jesus, just say the word and I know it will be done, because I know who You are.* Jesus is surrounded by people who want to believe but still struggle. Now He is meeting a man who has no such struggle, because he understands the essence of faith in someone else.

As much as we want to have answers to the many questions in our lives (and trust me, no one has more questions than me), God is calling us to a life of faith and radical obedience. Sometimes following Him is easy: "Did you see that, Jesus just fed five thousand people with a couple of fish and a loaf of bread!"

Sometimes following Him is hard: "This is a hard word, Jesus. I'm not sure I can do that."

And Jesus doesn't seem all that interested in clarity or certainty: "All these things Jesus said to the crowds in parables;

indeed, he said nothing to them without a parable" (Matt. 13:34). Keep in mind, even Jesus' disciples barely understood what all the parables meant, and they were constantly pulling Him aside to explain these strange stories. So they would get the inside scoop, but the thousands of others who heard His stories and didn't understand them? Sorry. You have to go home scratching your heads.

Does this mean that God doesn't care if we understand what He's saying or not? Of course not. If that were the case, Jesus never would have explained anything to the disciples. But I think Scripture makes it abundantly clear that God is not nearly as interested in giving us the full picture of things as He is in having us trust Him, no matter what we do or don't understand: "Unless you turn and become like children, you will never enter the kingdom of heaven" (Matt. 18:3).

I have three children, and the older they get, the less they trust their old man because they think they've got things figured out. When they were young, I could tell them not to do something and when they asked why, a simple "trust me on this one" would suffice. But now, as teenagers who know everything, my telling them not to do something without giving them a *very* good reason that aligns perfectly with their current worldview usually results in a lot of back and forth and wasted words, and possibly even disobedience, because they think they know better.

God has given us His Word to stand on when life gets crazy, when other worlds and other choices come crashing into ours and it no longer feels like God is with us or protecting us, and our idea of a loving God doesn't fit with the tragedy that has befallen us. Sometimes life just doesn't make sense, and short of God sitting us down for about ten years and systematically going through every decision that has been made for hundreds of years that has led up to this one moment in time when your world has been invaded by forces that are against you, well, we're just going to have to take Him at His word and trust Him.

> "For I know the plans I have for you," declares the LORD, "plans to prosper you and not to harm you, plans to give you hope and a future. Then you will call on me and come and pray to me, and I will listen to you. You will seek me and find me when you seek me with all your heart. I will be found by you," declares the LORD, "and will bring you back from captivity." (Jer. 29:11–14 NIV)

This is who God is. Whatever tragedies happen in your life, whatever decisions others make that hurt you deeply and will have ripple effects for generations to come, whatever poor decisions you yourself make that hurt you or others, this is who God is. His plans for us are always good, but more often than not we get in His way. But He is ever patient, ever kind, ever merciful, and ever full of grace for us and for those who bring pain into our lives. He is constantly working on our behalf, constantly waiting for us to call on Him so He can listen to us, find us, and set us free.

It's true that we're never going to have all the answers. But then again, maybe we don't need to. Maybe simple faith, despite how things look or seem, is enough. When we exercise faith like that, even Jesus is amazed. And that's not a bad place to start.

/9/

HE'LL MAKE THINGS DIFFICULT JUST TO PROVE A POINT

The story goes something like this: Someone is in dire need of money/food/supplies/you name it and if they don't get said money/food/supplies/you name it by such and such a date, they are going to lose their home/job/organization/you name it. All seems lost, because the thing that was needed never came and it's the night before it is needed. Then there is a knock on the door, a letter arrives, or some other unusual circumstance happens where whatever is needed arrives *just* in the nick of time, thus saving the home/job/organization/you name it. Once again, God comes through at the eleventh hour.

I usually experience two competing emotions every time I hear these amazing testimonies of God's provision. The first is amazement. I am as thirsty as anyone to see God move, and in moments like these He is so obviously present and real that I can't help but praise Him. But the second emotion I feel is frustration. Why does it seem like God *always* takes our needs to the very last minute before swooping in like Superman to save the day? It feels like He does stuff like this on purpose, makes things difficult and delayed, just to prove that He's God and we're not.

And it's not just stories of friends or missionaries that cause this frustration in me. There are loads of stories in the Bible that contribute.

SEEMS A LITTLE EXCESSIVE

My first Bible was probably my all-time favorite Bible ever. It was *The Picture Bible*, which broke the main stories down using a comic book format. I know they have other versions of this concept that are even cooler now, but back then, for a ten-year-old kid with little to no interest in God or churchy stuff, this book was pretty sweet. And like all the other kids my age, I spent most of my time with that picture Bible hanging out in the book of Judges.

Judges had everything a young boy getting his first drops of testosterone could want. Obviously, the gold standard was Samson, the Arnold Schwarzenegger of the Scriptures. Just thinking about him swinging that ox jaw bone around, killing three hundred guys on his own with it, still gives me all the feels. Samson was like the big dumb jock of the Bible—the strongest guy who ever lived but not really the sharpest. And if the idea of his having some sort of "magic hair" wasn't in the Bible, I would have thought that was a weak plot point. But there it was: dude got his strength from his hair. It's literally the only secret he had to keep, but when his lady friend puts on the charm, he messes with her a bit, trying to flirt, but ultimately caves and tells her what his kryptonite is. Men really haven't changed much.

Add to this the stories of Samson killing a lion with his bare hands, as well as tying three hundred foxes together, and finish the story with Samson getting his eyes gouged out and being forced into slave labor, followed by the fact that his hair is slowly growing back and everyone seems to forget that plot point, thus allowing him to go out in a blaze of glory as he topples a temple, killing three thousand Philistines and himself. This is primo stuff for a ten-year-old. It's like kid caviar.

While Samson may have been the main event, there are other crazy stories in the book of Judges. Like the lady who drove a tent peg through some guy's cranium while he slept; a dude who was so fat that when he was assassinated, his belly fat literally swallowed the sword; and the numbskull who won a battle and was so hyped up that he vowed to kill the first thing he saw when he returned home—which just happened to be his daughter. These weren't the stories I was getting in Sunday school, and a kid can only take so much deer-panting-for-the-water stuff before he snaps and dives into the book of Judges to get something a little juicier.

There was one story in Judges that didn't sit well, however, even though it was an incredible picture of God coming through in a big way.

Finally, Someone I Can Relate To

In Judges 6 we learn that because Israel (yet again) did evil in the sight of the Lord (it's like a broken record in Scripture), the

Lord gave them over to the Midianites for seven years. Basically, Israel is getting bullied. Anytime the Israelites planted crops, the Midianites would swoop in and take it all for themselves. They'd steal their sheep, their oxen, their donkeys, and their lunch money. And once Israel finally gets sick of getting atomic wedgies, they cry out to God for help. God hears their cries and comes up with a plan to save His kids.

God starts this plan off by picking His leader, who just so happens to be a coward who is the weakest in his family from the smallest tribe in Israel. When the Lord appears to Gideon, he's hiding out in a winepress, beating out wheat there to keep the Midianites from seeing what he's doing, like a kid hiding his lunch money in his shoe. Gideon is not striking the most promising pose of leadership.

But of course God doesn't see what man sees, and He greets Gideon by calling out his true identity: "The LORD is with you, O mighty man of valor" (Judg. 6:12). Gideon responds with a little bit of cheek that may actually hint toward the reservoir of bravery that only God seems to see right now: "Please, my lord, if the LORD is with us, why then has all this happened to us? And where are all his wonderful deeds that our fathers recounted to us . . . But now the LORD has forsaken us and given us into the hand of Midian" (Judg. 6:13).

Look at this guy. He may be hiding, but he's got a bit of a chip on his shoulder. *Oh yeah, the Lord is with me, huh? Sure doesn't look like it.* I think the aspect of God that amazes me the most is how patient He is with us. He's always so far ahead of the curve, and we always think we've got a solid handle on our situations. So when we say something stupid like this in our frustration, God responds in patience and grace. Look how God responds to this little shot: "And the LORD turned to him and said, '*Go in this might of yours* and save Israel from the hand of Midian; do I not send you?'" (Judg. 6:14).

The Lord sees the fury boiling below the surface and tells Gideon to use that to save Israel from the Midianites. *After all, if I'm sending you, it's all good.* This, of course, is *not* what Gideon was expecting, and he backtracks immediately.

"Please, Lord, how can I save Israel? Behold, my clan is the weakest in Manasseh, and I am the least in my father's house" (Judg. 6:15).

Then God reiterates what He just said.

"But I will be with you" (Judg. 6:16).

Those words are God's equivalent of a mic drop. What more can you say to Him when He tells you something like that? But our dear Gideon is not yet a mighty man of valor, so he does what many of us would probably do in that situation. He asks for a sign to show him who he's talking to. Gideon then asks the Lord to chill for a bit while he makes a meal, and what I just love about this is that God—posing as an angel, as He often did in the Old Testament—says no problem, I'll wait. And He just sits there waiting while Gideon cooks a meal! What a picture.

When Gideon brings the food out, the Lord tells him to put it on a rock. He then reaches out His staff and touches it, and the rock bursts into flames, consuming the meat and turning what was once a meal into an offering. Then God vanishes right in front of Gideon. I have no biblical proof for what I'm about to say, and I readily admit it comes only from my imagination, but I sure do hope God gave Gideon a little knowing wink right before He vanished.

After this, Gideon freaks out because he realizes he was

talking to God that whole time, but God tells him to relax, it's all good. But then He gives Gideon his first assignment as a "mighty man of valor." He wants Gideon to destroy an altar to Baal and build an altar to God on top of it. It's here we first see Gideon's internal flaw, and it speaks directly to the true identity God has called him to. Gideon did what God asked him to do, but he did it during the night "because he was too afraid of his family and the men of the town" (Judg. 6:27).

Gideon has a fear of man, and it will rise up again and again. We see it when he's threshing wheat in hiding, we see it here in his first task, and we'll see it again at his biggest moment. But it's important to note that often it's the things you fear the most that are going to be at the heart of God's call on your life. Gideon was small and fearful, but God was calling him to be strong and brave. I am about as introverted as you can get and don't like doing risky things, yet God's call on my life involves stepping into crazy situations with people and taking some of the biggest risks imaginable. There is a tension to God's call on our lives, a kind of yin and yang that I think is purposeful on God's part. In order to call us higher, we're going to have to overcome our biggest weaknesses, which we can really only do by abiding in Him.

All I ever wanted to be was a writer. It was the perfect job for me because it would allow me to live in my imagination and explore things in my mind without ever having to deal with other people. It was a solitary job, which suited me just fine. But God had plans for my life that far outstripped writing this book, and He needed to get me on board to do things I never would have signed up for on my own. And how did He do that? By showing me that what I was afraid of wasn't that bad and that I might actually be pretty good at what terrified me.

When I look back at my journey, it can be split up into roughly three equal parts. The first part was my learning how to tell a story. At the age of thirteen, I heard God's voice for the first time, and the only thing He said to me was that I was going to be a writer. Great! That's what I wanted to be anyway! But because my father was a professional artist, I was under no illusion as to how hard this was going to be. My shot at making a living by writing was a million-to-one, so I knew I was going to have to outwork everyone. So that's what I did. I immersed myself in the art of storytelling, of understanding an audience and how to structure something for maximum impact. I didn't have much of a life in high school and college, but I wasn't all that interested in "having a life." I just wanted to tell stories that mattered.

Phase two of God's plan for me was a three-in-one deal. I was making progress as a writer, but I couldn't communicate with people in real life at all. So at the age of twenty-three, through an interesting series of circumstances, I became a full-time college professor of, you guessed it, writing. Now I couldn't hide in my room anymore; I had to deal with real live people who didn't want to hear what I had to say and were only taking my class because their advisor was making them. But interestingly, I discovered almost immediately that I had a knack for speaking in front of people. So for the next thirteen years I honed my craft as a communicator.

The second thing teaching gave me was just enough cache to get my foot in the door with people I wanted to interview once I started making movies. I wasn't some crazy charismatic, I was a serious academic (lol) who wasn't going to make some weird, over-the-top film. Of course, that's exactly what I wound up doing with *Finger of God*, but I digress. The point is, I found that people tend to pay more attention to a fancy-pants college professor as opposed to some punk filmmaker.

The last thing teaching gave me was maybe the most important. During thirteen years of teaching, I read a truckload of terrible stories. I learned pretty early on that I wasn't going to be teaching many Shakespeares, and as much as reading the great novels of history and surrounding myself with some of the best books the world has to offer helped, I can definitely say that nothing taught me more about how to tell a good story than reading a boatload of bad stories. Teaching often focuses on showing students how to tell a good story, but for me, the teacher, I learned pretty much every way *not* to tell a story. So if the first third of my training ground was learning how to write the traditional way, the second part was like reverse engineering the writing process. I learned what good writing was by constantly seeing bad writing. Who knew that reading crummy student papers until your eyes bleed would be so effective?

Then, in phase three of God's plan to push me into my true destiny, I had to learn how to make movies. Before *Finger of God* I had never used video much, and I had to teach myself how to do everything while I was shooting that film. I'd be reading books on lighting while on the plane to some new place I was going to shoot. I used a book tutorial on editing *while* I was editing my feature film. I was about a week ahead of myself. And although my film and editing skills were about as raw as humanly possible, I did bring one thing to the process that the Lord had painstakingly curated in my life. He had taught me how to tell a good story.

Gideon was afraid of people, and he'd never done anything like what God was asking him to do, but Gideon did have one thing that served him well enough to carry out God's call on his life. Gideon wanted to see God move. There's a reason the first thing out of his mouth to the Lord was, "Where are all the wonderful deeds of God that I've heard about?" Gideon had a bent in his spirit to see God do great things, and that, probably more than anything, is what made him a mighty man of valor in God's eyes. Faith, remember, is the currency of heaven, and God saw a storehouse of riches beneath Gideon's fears and self-doubt.

But Gideon still has a ways to go. After he does his little nighttime Baal raid, the Midianites decide to ramp things up a bit against Israel, and they get some other punks, the Amalekites, to join forces to come lay waste to Israel. They enter Israel and cross the Jordan and then—well, something odd happens to Gideon. Obviously this kid's not quite ready for prime time, but since we're a little short on time, God gives him a little nudge:

> The Spirit of the LORD clothed Gideon, and he sounded the trumpet, and the Abiezrites were called out to follow him. And he sent messengers throughout all Manasseh, and they too were called out to follow him. And he sent messengers to Asher, Zebulun, and Naphtali, and they went up to meet them. (Judg. 6:34–35)

"The Spirit of the LORD *clothed* Gideon." When God touches you, your true identity comes forth whether you like it or not. God's touch lays waste to every fear because fear cannot abide in His presence. So the normal fears that keep Gideon hiding in winepresses disappear when God clothes him in His Spirit, and this "mighty man of valor" sounds the trumpet and puts out the call to Israel to rally to him and to God, to finally stand up and punch the bullies in the face.

How awesome would it be if God simply stayed all over Gideon and he was turned into some kind of action hero? But that's not really God's style. He's going to get done what He wants to get done, but He's also going to do what it takes to grow in friendship with you in the process. And sure enough, as soon as he undresses Himself from Gideon, the old fears and self-doubts fire up.

The end of Judges 6 shows Gideon perhaps at his worst. Maybe it's because he realizes there's no turning back now that he's put a call out to everyone and they're on their way to fight, but he's obviously tripping out in a big way. He falls back to his old "show me a sign" stuff, and once again, God overlooks his lack of faith to patiently deal with a hyperventilating war general.

Gideon needs to know *for sure* that God will be with him, so he lays out a fleece of wool and asks God to put dew on the fleece alone and keep the ground around it dry, which God does. But Gideon is in a really bad way, so he asks God to do it again but this time to reverse the dew. Let the wool be dry and the ground around it wet with dew. "God did so that night" (Judg. 6:40). I find it interesting that both of these miracles are done without a word from God. Maybe I'm reading too much into it, but I wonder if this severe lack of faith tested God's patience a bit. Or maybe it just set the stage for what was coming next, which is the true heart of the story. It's here that we catch a glimpse of the true heart of God, not only for Gideon, but also for us.

GIVE ME YOUR HAND

God's whittling down Gideon's men from thirty-two thousand to three hundred was one of those stories that, again, gave me mixed emotions. On the one hand it's a pretty awesome story because it's so absurd, but on the other hand it underlined my belief that God will make things way more difficult for us than they need to be just to, I don't know, show off that He's God. But of course, that's not what He's doing at all.

After Gideon gets his fleece on, it's time to go to work and crack some skulls. When everyone shows up after his summons, I'm sure Gideon feels pretty good about things, as there were thirty-two thousand men ready for battle. But then God throws cold water on him when He tells Gideon that there are way too many people here. God even tells Gideon where His mind is when He says, "The people with you are too many for me to give the Midianites into their hand, lest Israel boast over me, saying, 'My own hand has saved me'" (Judg. 7:2). God wants the credit for this victory, and overpowering numbers will only make Israel think they're responsible for their own salvation.

God tells Gideon to let anyone who's scared to fight go home, and a staggering two-thirds take off—twenty-two thousand men! So now Gideon is left with ten thousand, and God says it's still too many. So God gives Gideon a weird way to test the men and figure out who's going to war, but actually it's quite genius. He tells Gideon to have the men drink from the water and then watch how they do it.

Gideon is to separate the men by how they drink—either by cupping it in their hands and drinking or putting their entire faces down into the water. Only three hundred men cup the water (who the heck drinks by putting their face in the water? Apparently this was a thing back then), and these are the men God chooses to be Gideon's army. I used to think God just chose the lesser number because it was a smaller number, but then I learned an interesting tidbit. The men who cupped the water with their hands stayed ready for a fight because their eyes were always up. The men who dunked their heads to the water were vulnerable. So basically, God chose not only the smaller number, but the men who were instinctively the real warriors.

What happens next shows the mental mess Gideon's in:

> That same night the LORD said to him, "Arise, go down against the camp, for I have given it into your hand. But if you are afraid to go down, go down to the camp with Purah your servant. And you shall hear what they say, and afterward your hands shall be strengthened to go down against the camp." (Judg. 7:9–11)

There is no reason for God to do this for Gideon other than that Gideon's nerves are beyond frayed. It's pretty much go time, but God can see that Gideon is a mess. This "mighty man of valor" needs one more little push before he is ready to enter into true trust, true friendship with God. And the wonderful thing about this story is that God never holds Gideon's weakness against him. Instead, He holds his hand the entire time. *Come on Gideon, it's time to go win a war, to step into your full destiny and identity, but I get that you're afraid. So come on, grab your servant Purah and let's sneak down together so I can show you how trustworthy I am.*

So they sneak down to one of the outposts, and at that moment one of the guards is sharing a dream he had about their imminent destruction, and the other guard tells him, "This is no other than the sword of Gideon" (Judg. 7:14). And nothing is more important in this entire story than what happens next.

"As soon as Gideon heard the telling of the dream and its

interpretation, he worshiped" (Judg. 7:15). After all that—the initial call, the fleece, the whittling down of the soldiers—Gideon finally gets it. He finally understands what it means to trust God. He finally has eyes to see the goodness and faithfulness of the one who found a cowering runt and called him a mighty man of valor—and then turned him into one by pretty much doing everything for him. When you get to that place where God's faithfulness is laid bare and everything you've gone through makes sense, the only response you can have is to fall on your knees and worship Him.

I had a similar experience while filming one of my movies (minus the armies and killing and such) that was one of the many lessons God taught me as He slowly marched me toward a true friendship with Him. I was filming my third movie, *Father of Lights*, in India.

This was my second time filming in India, and this time we were filming with a man who often heard the Lord speaking to him in an audible voice. This was definitely new territory for me, but at this point I was knee-deep in discovering a very big God, so I went with it. While we were there, the Lord spoke to my friend and gave him a name and an address. That's it. No direction, nothing.

So he told me about this little note from God, and I immediately said let's go. But then he told me who this guy was, and I just stared at him. Apparently the man was a very well-known, very powerful witch doctor in the area, and he had even been known to curse people to death. My friend said it was odd that the Lord didn't tell us what to do, but that was all he had gotten. This was my film, it was up to me whether we wanted to have a little showdown with the witch doctor.

I have some friends who would hear that and without hesitation jump to their feet and yell, "Let's do it!" But I can assure you that my reaction was not one of jubilation. I didn't want to do this, but at the same time I had come here to make a film about God, and this sure seemed like something that would happen in a film about God. My first act was to email my wife and tell her the situation, find out if she didn't mind if her husband willingly went out to take on the forces of darkness. God spoke powerfully to her and she gave me the green light. Dang it. I was hoping that would go differently. Okay then, I suppose let's do it. We planned to drive to the address the next day.

That night I was awakened at 2:00 a.m. with what I can only describe as a demonic atmosphere in my room. The air was thick with fear, and I've never felt anything like the terror and dread I felt as I sat in the darkness, hearing dogs barking in the alley outside, thinking about what we were going to do the next day. It was wild, irrational fear, but a fear so deep in my bones that I almost threw up. I lay in my bed praying desperately until I fell asleep again. One of my greatest regrets as a filmmaker is not turning the camera on myself to give the viewer a glimpse of what was going on inside me. I'd have probably looked like a weirdo, but I know the emotion would have been palpable.

The next day we filmed in a separate village (I call it the "machete village" in the movie), then we drove about twenty minutes or so before we pulled over on the side of the road. There was a tiny village of maybe six or eight houses we walked through, and they all seemed abandoned. We then walked on a dirt path that wound through trees and shrubbery and all of a sudden we were at the door of a dingy little hut.

Inside was a man in a white tanktop. It was evening, and

he had no lights on in his hut. He sat on his bed and he started shouting things as soon as we walked up. I didn't speak the language, so I had no idea what was going on. Plus, I was too busy dealing with my own fears, wanting to just call off this whole thing and go home. But here I was, cameras rolling, on my hands and knees at his doorway trying to get a decent shot of what was going on inside as we stayed just outside trying to talk to him. I was as tensed up as I've ever been, and I sat there praying under my breath for God to protect us, show up, do something, please.

Finally I looked up at my friend who was talking to the man, asking him questions in a language I didn't understand. I whispered a weak, "What's going on?" He turned to me and said, "He doesn't want us to come in. He's afraid of us now."

It was as if someone had pulled a plug in my spirit. Instantly every feeling of fear left, replaced by the place God was trying to get me to through this entire ordeal. Faith. Sweet, pure, trusting faith. God had done it. The fight I was dreading didn't even happen because God had gone ahead of us and fought our battle for us. We would later find out that two hours before our arrival the witch doctor had somehow "lost his powers," which is why he was hiding out in his hut, terrified of us. When we approached, he knew we were the reason his powers had gone. I looked in the doorway again and saw a shell of a man, rocking back and forth on his bed, pleading with us to go away.

It was a defining moment for me, and I got just a tiny glimpse of what Gideon must have felt when he, too, was peeking at someone, a soldier, and heard that God had already gone before him and the battle was over before it started.

Why did God do things the way He did with me during those two days? Why didn't He keep the fear at bay the night before, allowing me to sleep peacefully and then showing His power the next day without putting me through all that? Certainly He could have, but I can honestly say it wouldn't have had nearly the effect on me that this set of events did. I was paralyzed by fear, and I was desperate for God to do something. He needed to show me it was Him and Him alone who would direct, guide, and protect me as I made these films. It wasn't the greatness of the people I was filming with, or my amazing faith. It was, and always would be, Him.

God is well aware that His invisibility is a massive hindrance to us being able to believe in Him, trust Him, and in turn, love Him. So when He moves on our behalf, when He protects or provides for us, He often will do it in a way that for the briefest moment causes a rip in that invisibility cloak of His. When that check arrives at the eleventh hour, when that job offer comes out of nowhere when all seems lost, when that witch doctor is silenced before you even show up, that's when you can see God most clearly—you see His character, His love for you, His desire to bless you, and you do the only thing you can do when you finally catch a glimpse of God.

You worship Him.

I used to be afraid of God because it seemed like He was always doing things or causing complications in my life just to prove some point about how great He is. But that was a very unfair view of the situation and of God's role in my life. God may delay an answer, but He only does this so we can see Him more clearly, like a ripple in a reflective glass hinting that someone else is on the other side of that glass. The overpowering nature of His glory keeps Him from being able to show Himself clearly and openly, because our choice to love and trust Him must come from a place of complete freedom. So He works with what He's been given and proves Himself over and over again by never allowing us to fall, even though He catches us right before we *do* fall. But He doesn't do it this way to show off, He does it this way to show Himself to us.

We don't like God doing things this way, because it's stressful. We just want Him to do His God stuff earlier so we don't have to fuss and worry about our lives. But that reveals more about us than it does God. The Lord has already made it clear what He wants us to do:

Do not be anxious about anything, but in every situation, by prayer and petition, with thanksgiving, present your requests to God. And the peace of God, which transcends all understanding, will guard your hearts and your minds in Christ Jesus. (Phil. 4:6–7 NIV)

Therefore I tell you, do not worry about your life, what you will eat or drink; or about your body, what you will wear. Is not life more than food, and the body more than clothes? Look at the birds of the air; they do not sow or reap or store away in barns, and yet your heavenly Father feeds them. Are you not much more valuable than they? Can any one of you by worrying add a single hour to your life?

And why do you worry about clothes? See how the flowers of the field grow. They do not labor or spin. Yet I tell you that not even Solomon in all his splendor was dressed like one of these. If that is how God clothes the grass of the field, which is here today and tomorrow is thrown into the fire, will he not much more clothe you—you of little faith? So do not worry, saying, 'What shall we eat?' or 'What shall we drink?' or 'What shall we wear?' For the pagans run after all these things, and your heavenly Father knows that you need them. But seek first his kingdom and his righteousness, and all these things will be given to you as well. Therefore do not worry about tomorrow, for tomorrow will worry about itself. Each day has enough trouble of its own. (Matt. 6:25–34 NIV)

I am a father to three children, and as a father, there are a few different ways I interact with my kids. Sometimes I just want to enjoy their company. Sometimes I want to teach them something about life or love. Sometimes I want to push them to be better. Sometimes I have to keep my mouth shut while they bump into walls in their own journeys toward faith, because some lessons can only be learned by living. I don't think our experience with God is much different. Sometimes He just wants us to abide with Him and to enjoy each other's presence. Sometimes He wants to lavish us with gifts. Sometimes He wants to protect us from something, but sometimes He may see the benefit—*our* benefit—in having us go through something hard. God always approaches us as a Father, and all good fathers want the best for their kids.

The story of Gideon is the story of a patient, loving Father seeing the greatness in a man that no one else can see, then patiently and methodically walking with him toward that greatness, dealing with his fears and issues along the way. He never once makes Gideon feel like an idiot for not trusting Him enough, nor does He punish Gideon for wrestling with his own faith. Instead, He walks with, guides, and, yes, even pushes Gideon to a place that reveals to Gideon what God saw all along but that also drives the two of them into a deeper place of trust, a deeper friendship.

Friendship, faith, trust—that's always the endgame for God. Always.

/10/

HE IS SELFISH

I know it may sound a little weird to call God selfish (He did, after all, sacrifice His only Son to offer salvation to everyone), but of all the misconceptions I had about God and perhaps the one that lodged itself most firmly in my crazed notions of who God was, this was the biggie. Not only did I think He was selfish, I thought He was the most selfish person in the universe.

My reasoning for this was simple. Everything was always about Him. Everything I did in life was supposed to be for Him. If you didn't choose to believe in and serve Him, you were going to be punished by being thrown into hell, and all He seemed to care about was people obeying Him. I mean, He was God and I wasn't, so there wasn't much I could do about any of this other than believe the right stuff and try to obey Him as best I could. I had the mentality that yeah, I had to put up with life on His terms because He was the all-powerful one, but hey, at least I got heaven out of the deal and that place was supposed to be the bomb. So faith became more of an exercise in placating a benevolent tyrant whose Son was really cool so that I could get a sweet mansion in a dope location when I died.

I had loads of biblical stuff to back me up, so this was never really something I struggled with much. It's just the way things were. Apparently God was so powerful and so holy that He deserved all the worship and accolades He demanded. I just thought it was kind of weird that He straight up asked for them. Seemed a little needy to me. I honestly used to think that God just kind of existed to suck up our praise like some giant cosmic vacuum cleaner.

In case you haven't figured it out yet, I had issues.

Remember that verse in Romans 9 that we looked at earlier, where Paul is making the faux argument that if God always planned on you doing something naughty, then how could He hold it against you when you were naughty? And the answer was the very unsatisfying "Who do you think you are to question God?" Yeah, that verse was pretty much ground zero for my dysfunctional thinking. But it certainly wasn't my only ammo.

USING DEATH TO SHOW OFF

One of my all-time favorite Bible verses is John 11:35. I attended a Lutheran elementary school as a kid, and we had a religion class that was basically just a class where we had to memorize Bible verses. It's probably where I first started disliking the word *religion*. I hated having to memorize Bible verses, mostly because they weren't written in normal English but had this weird cadence, there were enormous run-on sentences, and they contained words like *thee* and *thou*. And you had to get every word right, otherwise you'd be docked. It was really stressful for a ten-year-old, and probably not the best introduction to the Word of God.

Once in a while, though, the teacher would allow us to choose our own Bible verse. It became a mad scramble to be the first one to submit either John 3:16 or John 11:35: "Jesus wept."

That verse was a thing of beauty to a kid who hated having to memorize stuff. I mean, just two words? It's not like they were amazing words either. They were just two words telling me that Jesus cried. Okay. So? Why is this earth-shattering news? I guessed it was because it was Jesus, and since Jesus was so serious all the time, His crying was, like, something really strange. Not going to lie, I never read the whole story as a kid. I just wanted to use the verse to feed my own scholastic laziness.

As I got older, I became more familiar with the story surrounding this verse, and even though it was an incredible story and had some cool elements a kid like me would like (Lazarus had been dead for four days, I wonder if his flesh was starting to peel off!), and it showed that Jesus was the ultimate spiritual power hitter, there was something about the story that didn't sit right with me.

I often wondered if Jesus ever got sick of sick people. Most of the stories in the Gospels involve Jesus healing the sick and casting out demons—it was probably the main reason He became so famous. Sure He taught the Scriptures with power and authority, but if people back then were anything like people today, the preaching was just the required listening before the real show could begin.

The sick man is Lazarus, a friend of Jesus. In fact, we've met this family before in Luke 10:38–42. When Jesus enters a certain village, Martha, Lazarus's sister, welcomes Jesus into her house for a potluck. Jesus apparently gets on a roll and starts teaching, and Martha's sister, Mary, sits at Jesus' feet soaking it all in. Martha gets all huffy because she has to do all the work while her sis lounges around, and she even goes so far as to whine about it to Jesus.

What a scene that must have been. I wonder if she actually interrupted Jesus, all sweaty and flustered, hair askew, sounding grumpy as she said, "Lord, do you not care that my sister has left me to serve alone? Tell her then to help me" (Luke 10:40). She whines to Jesus! I wonder if people are allowed to read Scripture in heaven, and if Martha smacks her head in embarrassment every time she reads that line? Anyway, there's no mention of Lazarus in this encounter. Either he's in the living room listening, or he's in the backyard watching the ball game, letting his sisters do their "religious stuff."

Whatever Lazarus was doing that day, the three of them became good friends with Jesus. We know Jesus and Lazarus are tight when, in the story we're now looking at, both sisters send for Jesus, saying, "He whom you love is ill" (John 11:3). So we're talking about good friends of Jesus, and one of those friends is suffering. When word reaches Jesus, though, He responds: "This illness does not lead to death. It is for the glory of God, so that the Son of God may be glorified through it" (John 11:4).

Now that sounds all good and religious and like the Bible, but what Jesus is saying is, "It's all good, I've got this covered. I'm just going to chill here for a while." Strangely, the next verse reiterates Jesus' love for this family: "Now Jesus loved Martha and her sister and Lazarus. So, when he heard that Lazarus was ill, he stayed two days longer in the place where he was" (John 11:5–6).

Jesus loves this family a lot, and He also knows what He is going to do. As a token of His love for the family, He decides to stay put two days longer, apparently to make sure Lazarus is really dead and not just mostly dead. Jesus is a way bigger deal than Miracle Max in *The Princess Bride*, after all.

This little admission from Jesus was a big-time issue for me and speaks directly to the idea of God's selfishness that I harbored for years.

When I read the Word, especially the Gospels, I am constantly fighting the temptation to just read everything quickly, think *Yep, it's still the same*, and check off a box on my daily devotional list. When I feel this thinking settling in, I usually try to slow down and get further into the story by trying to discover details I haven't seen before.

For the longest time I just moved right through the story of Lazarus, knowing that Jesus was gearing up for one of His main event miracles. But when I stopped to really examine it, I found it a bit troubling.

If you've ever been around someone who is desperately ill, close to death, you know that it is not a pleasant experience. I have had friends and family members who suffered greatly from physical ailments or sickness, begging God to relieve them of their suffering. Sometimes He did, but usually they either had to learn to live with it or modern medicine was used to help ease the pain. The point is, Lazarus, Jesus' friend, is suffering badly. His sisters make a call to Jesus to come help, knowing full well that all Lazarus needs is for Jesus to show up. But Jesus' response is to wait.

Let him suffer.

Let him die.

"For the glory of God, so that the Son of God may be glorified though it."

When you're already struggling with the notion of God's goodness and heart for you, a story like this is a punch to the gut. Jesus always planned to heal Lazarus, but He decides to go the route of maximum anguish, heartache, and sadness before He'll do it. The whole point of His waiting, after all, is to make sure Lazarus dies.

When I say I believed God was selfish, this is what I'm talking about. He may heal you, but it's going to be on His terms, and He's going to do it in a way that is most impressive. It doesn't matter that you have to suffer more, because it's all about His getting glory. And if more suffering brings Him more glory, well then doggone it, you're going to suffer more.

I picture Lazarus on his death bed, reality settling in that Jesus, his good friend, the one so full of love and compassion who healed everyone who called on His name, isn't going to show up for him. Jesus isn't coming. His sisters sit next to Lazarus, weeping quietly, both wondering where Jesus is—why hasn't He come? Their messenger returns telling them that Jesus got their request to come, yet He decided not to. Is He still our friend? Is He angry with us? Did we do something wrong?

And then Lazarus takes his last, rattling breath. And the women weep. And funeral arrangements have to be made. And sorrow hangs over the house as everything reminds them of their brother. And well-wishers stop by, trying to help but only making it worse by reminding them of the tragedy. The numbness of it all sets in, and Martha cooks to keep herself busy while Mary sits in her room and cries. Unspoken through it all is the question: Why didn't Jesus show up?

Perhaps the most frequent prayer I have prayed in my lifetime, especially surrounding sickness and suffering, has simply been, "Lord, this is absolutely nothing for You. A snap of Your fingers. Not even that, a mere breath, a mere thought from You would heal them." And when nothing happens and the suffering continues, your mind starts to go down some very dark roads, and you begin to wonder if God has abandoned you, or if He doesn't really care, or if He is even real.

Eventually, Jesus heads out to visit His friends. He knows what He's about to encounter, because He tells His disciples that Lazarus is dead. By the time He shows up, Lazarus has been in the tomb for four days, and Mary and Martha are surrounded by friends who have come to console them. The funeral has already taken place. Mary and Martha are told that Jesus is coming, that He's near. Martha drops what she's doing and rushes to Him. Mary, on the other hand, stays seated in the house. Mary, remember, is the emotional one. Her staying seated speaks volumes. She loves Jesus, but at this moment she is angry at Him. Or disappointed. Or maybe a combination of both. All we know for certain is that Mary is not okay. Maybe she doesn't trust herself and what she would say to Him. Maybe bitterness is seeping into her. *You heal everyone else who comes to You, but You won't even come in time to heal one of Your best friends?*

When Martha reaches Jesus, her first words tell us everything we need to know. "Lord, if you had been here, my brother would not have died" (John 11:21).

There is a hint of accusation there. She wants to ask Him where He's been, but there is too much respect for Jesus to do that. What Martha says next shows that maybe she'd been paying attention to the Master while she'd been so busy feeding Him:

"But even now I know that whatever you ask from God, God will give you" (John 11:22).

Is she hinting that she believes Jesus could raise her brother from the dead? She's certainly dancing around the thought. Jesus' response could be taken a few different ways. God is always presenting us with moments of choice for our faith. He has often given me peace for a situation or a decision, but rarely does He give me full clarity of what is to come. Clarity is not God's currency; faith is. So He constantly charges our account, trying to see if we will spend our faith currency on Him.

"Your brother will rise again" (John 11:23).

What does that mean? Is Jesus responding to Martha's hint at resurrection? Or is He offering up some future hope to a grieving friend? Martha seems to take it as the latter, and we see her previous hope-filled faith wither a bit. Of course it was too much to hope for. "Martha said to him, 'I know that he will rise again in the resurrection on the last day'" (John 11:24).

Then Jesus gives her one of His—well, I call them "Jesus-isms." Jesus is the most creative person who ever walked the earth, and He often gave responses to people that, while not being direct answers to a specific question, provided a chance for teaching and revelation. To someone who just wants a clear answer, though, they can be frustratingly vague. "Jesus said to her, 'I am the resurrection and the life. Whoever believes in me, though he die, yet shall he live, and everyone who lives and believes in me shall never die. Do you believe this?'" (John 11:25–26).

Jesus knows what Martha wants to hear. He knows what she's asking Him to do. He also knows that He is going to do exactly that. But instead of saying, "Don't worry, Martha, I'm here to raise Lazarus from the dead," He speaks, not just to her and this moment, but also to all of us—the whole world, in fact. His final question to Martha is interesting. "Do you believe this?" Jesus gave Martha a chance to exercise her faith when He told her, "Your brother will rise again." She backed down from radical faith then, so He now talks about who He is and the core of what He offers to everyone, including her dead brother.

Martha passes the next test with flying colors. She may be frustrated, angry, and confused, but she will not let those emotions get in the way of the rock solid truth she believes. She says, "Yes, Lord; I believe that you are the Christ, the Son of God, who is coming into the world" (John 11:27).

Curiously, Martha then leaves Jesus to get Mary. "When she had said this, she went and called her sister Mary, saying in private, 'The Teacher is here and is calling for you.' And when she heard it, she rose quickly and went to him. Now Jesus had not yet come into the village, but was still in the place where Martha had met him" (John 11:28–30).

Mary had no desire to go meet Jesus when she first heard He was coming. But now, when her sister tells her Jesus is calling for her, she "rises quickly" and goes to Him. What is happening here? Why doesn't Jesus just follow Martha into the village and to the house to see Mary?

We can only guess, but Jesus is always aware of what He's doing and why He's doing it, so we can surmise that there is purpose in this. I think it is safe to assume that Jesus is fully aware of Mary's anger and frustration and hurt toward Him, simply from the fact that Mary didn't accompany Martha to greet Him. Maybe Martha mentioned as much to Him and it wasn't recorded. Whatever the case, He's Jesus, so He definitely knows what's up. I wonder if He is giving her another chance to come to Him, an act of mercy and grace, perhaps?

Inherent with God is an invitation. He is always extending an invitation to approach Him, to come to Him, and to seek Him out. Here is just a sample:

If my people who are called by my name humble themselves, and pray and *seek my face* and turn from their wicked ways, then I will hear from heaven and will forgive their sin and heal their land. (2 Chron. 7:14)

I love those who love me, and *those who seek me diligently* find me. (Prov. 8:17)

For I know the thoughts that I think toward you, says the LORD, thoughts of peace and not of evil, to give you a future and a hope. Then *you will call upon Me* and go and pray to Me, and I will listen to you. And *you will seek Me* and find Me, *when you search for Me with all your heart.* (Jer. 29:11–13 NKJV)

Come to Me, all you who labor and are heavy laden, and I will give you rest. (Matt. 11:28 NKJV)

Let us therefore *come boldly to the throne of grace*, that we may obtain mercy and find grace to help in time of need. (Heb. 4:16 NKJV)

Draw near to God and He will draw near to you. (James 4:8 NKJV)

For whatever reason, God wants us to approach Him. This isn't an "I sit on my throne and you must grovel your way to me" or even a "you're too insignificant for me to come to you" situation. God doesn't *need* us; He simply *wants* us. But we, on the other hand, *need* Him. Our problem is that most of the time we don't want Him despite our need of Him.

This entire book, and all Christianity, centers around a relationship between God and man. Relationships are two-sided. One person cannot be the only one pursuing or approaching or giving or receiving. God's love is grounded in freedom, and He is always extending an invitation, but it is an invitation that must be *acted* upon by us.

Jesus knows Mary is upset, and He also understands why. As we shall soon see, God is not some coldhearted deity. He is a God of empathy. He understands us, and He stoops to our emotional level because He loves us.

So Jesus calls to Mary, as He calls to all of us in our times of distress, anger, and pain. How we respond reflects the state of our faith, not who God is. Some, like the seed thrown on rocky ground in Jesus' parable of the sower in Matthew 13, see their faith fall away "when trouble or persecution comes" (NIV). Jesus is asking Mary, *Even though you are in pain, angry, and confused by what has happened, will you still come to Me when I call?*

Mary may be emotional but her faith is strong, and she responds to Jesus' call by going straight to him. She collapses at His feet, her sadness winning out over her attempt at strength and dignity, and she weeps. She also says the very same thing her sister said to Him. "Lord, if you had been here, my brother would not have died" (John 11:32).

Mary is a broken woman. Her friends are also weeping. Their sadness is palpable. Jesus has just walked into an atmosphere of raw, guttural grief. What He does in response defies logic.

> When Jesus saw her weeping, and the Jews who had come with her also weeping, he was deeply moved in his spirit and greatly troubled. And he said, "Where have you laid him?" They said to him, "Lord, come and see." Jesus wept. (John 11:33–35)

On the surface this makes perfect sense. Jesus sees everyone crying, so He cries too. It's a natural human reaction to cry when other people cry. But that isn't what's happening here.

Jesus knows why He is here, and He knows that in about ten minutes, everyone who is now crying will be laughing and rejoicing. Mary will fall even more in love with him—so much so that just before He goes to the cross, she will pour a bottle of perfume worth nearly fifty thousand dollars on his feet and wipe it up with her hair, both things so extravagant that they were considered scandalous. Jesus knows that He will be dining with Lazarus tonight. Why then does He weep?

The key to understanding why Christ weeps is found in the beginning of the verse. "When Jesus saw her weeping, and the Jews who had come with her also weeping, *he was deeply moved in his spirit and greatly troubled.*" Emotion is building inside Jesus, not because His friend is dead, but because of the pain and sorrow He sees in His other friends.

Then He asks to see the tomb. When they begin to take him to where Lazarus is buried, that's when Jesus finally breaks and begins to weep. He is aware of the pain and suffering His decision to wait has caused Mary and Martha and their friends, and it moves Him deeply. But He is perhaps most aware of what His friend Lazarus has endured. As they move toward the tomb, God's heart is revealed in full. This event had to happen, but that doesn't mean it didn't take something from Jesus to do it. And He now weeps for what Mary, Martha, and Lazarus have gone through. He weeps for the pain they have endured. He weeps for the pain that, in no small part, He caused.

God will never allow His foreknowledge to get in the way of His relationship with us. It is for this reason that He weeps when we weep and rejoices when we rejoice. Jesus wept because He was fully present in that moment. Sure He understood that in a short while weeping would turn to laughter, but Jesus cares about us *now*, in this moment, as much as He cares about what is to come. While God certainly works toward an endgame, He also stays with us through it all, the Great Comforter and Friend.

We see, as Jesus approaches the tomb, that He is "deeply moved again" (v. 38). This is the picture of a man filled with grief, filled with compassion. His emotion is not a one-time, brief, in-the-moment reaction to the sorrow of His friends. It is real and it is painful. God is moved by us. He is moved by you.

Getting Personal

I've never experienced this more clearly than during the hardest season of my life. It felt like everything was crashing down around me, and sorrow followed me everywhere. I cried every day for months. I begged God for relief, begged Him to intervene, begged Him to stand up and do something. I pouted, I screamed, I even went so low as to throw an "after all I've done for you" outburst at Him. This was pain like I've never felt, a shaking of everything in my life that I loved and believed.

Around this time, I was shooting season two of my two televisions shows, *Adventures with God* and *Questions with God*, and I was flying in around twenty friends and ministry people I'd filmed with over the years for the roundtable discussions we'd be shooting. Before I went down to Orlando where we'd be hanging out and shooting for a week, I prayed and asked God to give me a word from someone—to bring me some relief. And after a moment's hesitation, I just went for it.

"And I'd like it to come from Shawn Bolz, please."

Shawn is a good friend of mine, and in my opinion he is one of the healthiest and strongest prophetic voices in ministry today. I needed to hear from the Lord, and I needed it from someone I trusted.

Shawn wasn't yet aware of what was going on in my life because I was waiting to see him in person to talk to him about it. So you can imagine my surprise when, shortly after he arrived in Orlando, he pulled me aside because he had something to tell me. Sweet relief flooded me. The Lord had heard my cry. Finally God was going to tell me what He was going to do, how He was going to fix this. Finally I'd get a word from the Lord, a promise I could hold onto.

Shawn looked at me with concern on his face. Then, he spoke. "Hey, Darren, I don't know what's going on in your life right now, but the Lord gave me a clear word to give to you. He wants you to know that He's grieving with you."

I stared at him. "Is that it?"

"Yeah, that's what I heard on the way over here for you."

I don't think I've ever been more disappointed or, quite

frankly, more angry at God than I was right there, standing with Shawn Bolz, a puzzled look on his face. *Really, God? That's the big word You had for me? You're grieving with me? Big deal! Everyone is grieving with me! I don't need You to cry for me, I need You to do something! I need You to stand up and be God, fix this situation, do what only You can do!*

I was angry at God for a solid six months after that. Well, maybe *angry* is too strong. Disappointment was my primary emotion. At my lowest point, I needed Jesus to show up, and instead all He did was stand on the sidelines and cry.

But then God began to heal my heart. He began to meet me in ways I wasn't expecting. He began to pull me out of this wilderness I was lost in and bring me into a new day, where hope and happiness once again felt like things that were real and might even exist for me again. He shook my entire world to see what would be left standing, and in the process I learned a lot about what I really believed, who I really was, what my faith was really made of, if I truly had a heart of love, and, most important, who He was. This book is the result of that season of shaking.

It became clear to me months after this word from Shawn that in my time of deepest suffering, I wanted relief. I wanted the suffering to stop. I wanted a God who would fix it. But the reality was that in my time of deepest suffering, I actually didn't need an Almighty God who would fix things. I needed a friend who would sit with me in my sorrow. And when the Lord told me that He was grieving with me, He was showing me that He was my friend. He knows how it's all going to turn out. He could see the joy that would once again come into my life. He knew He was going to make all things beautiful. But at that moment, He saw

His friend crying and in pain, and He was deeply moved. Jesus looked at me in my suffering, and Jesus wept.

———

How do we deal with Jesus being willing to allow us to suffer so that "the Son of God may be glorified through it"? Well, we can probably start by understanding and accepting that once again, the world doesn't revolve around us. The world revolves around God, and God's great pursuit is to get His kids back—to save them from death and destruction and bring them back into a right relationship with Him. "Many of the Jews therefore, who had come with Mary and had seen what [Jesus] did, believed in him" (John 11:45).

Jesus is everything. The will of God is everything. If you think that's a cop-out, then you don't really know God. There comes a point in life when you have to realize how unimportant you are in the grand scheme of things and how much of a miracle it is that the God of the universe cares about you. He cares about your situation, your needs, your problems. He'll even go so far as to grieve with you, simply because He knows you are in pain. But make no mistake, He is God and you are not. "For my thoughts are not your thoughts, neither are your ways my ways, declares the LORD. For as the heavens are higher than the earth, so are my ways higher than your ways and my thoughts than your thoughts" (Isa. 55:8–9).

Is God selfish? Of course not. Inherent in selfishness is sinfulness and self-absorption and pride. God is love, remember? Love is the opposite of selfish. Love is patient and kind. It does not envy, it does not boast, it is not proud. It does not dishonor others, and *it is not self-seeking.*

The problem with thinking that God is selfish because He allows things in our lives to bring glory to Him is that this thinking is rooted in our own pride and arrogance. I used to get offended by the idea of God flat-out stating that we need to worship Him because He is worthy of our worship. But that's the whole point. He *is* worthy of our worship! He *does* deserve the highest praise. We must bow to Him because He is holy. We bow because He is love. We bow because He is our King.

We can look at this in one of two ways. In one version, Jesus simply used Lazarus to get more people to believe in Him. That's the way I viewed it for most of my life. In that version, God is an adversary of sorts. He's someone to be feared because of the power He wields and what He can do to you that would hurt. You only believe you are being used by someone when that relationship isn't strong. People in a true, loving relationship never use each other for their own gain. That is only done by unhealthy people.

When I questioned God about how He treated Lazarus, I was doing so out of my own fears and issues, because in truth I did see Him as an adversary. I never believed He was on my side. But then I became friends with Him and began to get a greater understanding of His heart not just for humanity, but for me personally. Jesus did what He did with Lazarus because it needed to be done. For us to reduce that entire episode to being about a few more people simply believing in Jesus is to once again err in thinking that we can have even the tiniest understanding of why things happen.

What matters is not so much what Jesus does and how it affects Lazarus, Mary, and Martha. What matters are Jesus' actions toward His friends. Yes, God has a lot on His plate, and, yes, He has full understanding of the millions of plates spinning in different directions while we are undergoing our one little moment of pain. But His enormity doesn't keep Him from taking the time to invite us back into His arms, meeting us right where we are, and walking alongside us fully present and emotionally invested.

God isn't selfish, but we are. We want God to meet all our needs and answer all our prayers the way we want them answered. We want Him to protect us from everything bad and painful. We want the world to revolve around us. But it never will, and God loves too many others to ever allow that to happen. We are the ones who are self-centered, not God. That doesn't mean the pain we feel in tragedy or hardships isn't real. It's very important to God, which is why He will always come alongside and weep with you.

And the one promise we can stand on, even in the midst of the storm, is that "*in all things* God works for the good of those who love him" (Rom. 8:28 NIV). He will stand with you, walk with you, and weep with you for sure. But He will never leave you in that place.

A resurrection is coming.

/11/

HE IS SILENT

I have a lot of friends who say they talk to God. Like conversational, back-and-forth talking, not just speaking into the void and hoping you're being heard talking. While I can say with some trepidation that I, too, talk with God, I wouldn't call it a torrential waterfall of conversation, but rather more of a nice, trickling stream. The Lord speaks to me in a variety of ways. Sometimes it's in my thoughts, sometimes it's in my body, sometimes it's through dreams, and sometimes it's through other people.

That being said, my friends who talk to God a lot all say that sometimes God goes silent. This is perhaps the most common frustration I hear from people wanting a relationship with the Lord. For some, it seems like He's always silent. They're trying to hear from Him, but nothing ever gets through. For others, myself included, they sometimes enter into seasons of hardship, made worse by the fact that they can't hear the Lord anymore. It's as if He just bailed right when everything started to get tough.

For someone who wants a relationship with me, it seems like

it would be much easier if God weren't so difficult to hear. Yes, I can hear Him in the still, small voice, but I guess I want to know why it has to be a small voice in the first place. When God revealed Himself to Elijah on the mountain, He wasn't in the wind or the earthquake or the fire, but in the silence (1 Kings 19). That's fine, I guess, but sometimes it would be nice to hear a shout rather than a whisper.

> It is the glory of God to conceal a matter; to search out a matter is the glory of kings. (Prov. 25:2 NIV)

> At that very time He rejoiced greatly in the Holy Spirit, and said, "I praise You, O Father, Lord of heaven and earth, that You have hidden these things from the wise and intelligent and have revealed them to infants. Yes, Father, for this way was well-pleasing in Your sight." (Luke 10:21 NASB)

As a filmmaker who is a Christian, it saddens me that most of our faith-based films are so overt in their messaging. While I get the intent—you want to make sure people really understand and value the *point* of your story—it typically has the opposite effect on people. Great art is almost never overt. When you have to do almost no work to get something, its value is diminished. But when you must work for something, you value it much more, and typically your enjoyment increases as well.

I love seafood, and high on my list of favorites are crab legs and lobster. Lobster is great because it all comes out pretty easily in one big chunk. Crab legs, on the other hand, require a little work to get to the meat inside, and while I love eating lobster, there's nothing quite like digging out that annoyingly difficult piece of crab meat. You feel like you've triumphed a little bit with crab legs. With lobster, you're just full.

Apparently God is not as concerned with people understanding Him as we are with people understanding us. Jesus is a perfect example: "All these things Jesus said to the crowds in parables; indeed, he said nothing to them without a parable" (Matt. 13:34).

Time and time again in the Gospels, Jesus speaks in parables and afterward His disciples come to Him to ask what the heck He was talking about. His disciples! Imagine how the poor guy sitting in the field listening to Jesus speak who didn't have private access to Jesus felt. And when His disciples press Jesus as to why He does it this way, His answer is not one you'd often hear from modern-day pastors.

> The disciples came to him and asked, "Why do you speak to the people in parables?"
>
> He replied, "Because the knowledge of the secrets of the kingdom of heaven has been given to you, but not to them. Whoever has will be given more, and they will have an abundance. Whoever does not have, even what they have will be taken from them. This is why I speak to them in parables:
>
> "Though seeing, they do not see;
>> though hearing, they do not hear or understand.
> In them is fulfilled the prophecy of Isaiah:
>> "'You will be ever hearing but never understanding;
>> you will be ever seeing but never perceiving.
> For this people's heart has become calloused;
>> they hardly hear with their ears,
>> and they have closed their eyes.

Otherwise they might see with their eyes,
　　hear with their ears,
　　understand with their hearts
　　and turn, and I would heal them."

(MATT. 13:10–15 NIV)

Jesus is very clear here. *I speak this way so the people who are open to what I am saying will receive and understand it.* The phrase "he who has ears, let him hear" is used sixteen times in the New Testament. There seems to be something in God's character that wants to hide things for those who want to find them. While this goes against most Western evangelical thinking—we want to make sure everyone perfectly understands everything—it actually makes sense.

The artist Marc Chagall said, "A thing must be elusive if it is ever to acquire its true identity." And I think the same holds true with the truths of the kingdom of God. The kingdom of God is upside down: The first are last and the last are first, the greatest among you must be the most humble servant, wisdom is hidden from the wise and given to infants. It is the hiddenness of the kingdom that makes it so potent, because when your eyes are opened and you finally see, it's as if something inside your spirit is unlocked and you can never unsee.

When I was a teenager getting really serious about the craft of writing, my family couldn't afford a computer so I used to write on a word processor. For those of you who just stared at those two words wondering what on earth they mean, let me explain. Back in ancient times, people used to have to write on typewriters. The word processor was the next step in the evolutionary chain of typewriting. For the first time, writing was digital, but you could only look at three or four lines at a time as you wrote them. My word processor looked like a typewriter with a little LED screen that showed me the words I was writing. Anyway, I wrote a *ton* of stuff on that thing, but it was annoying as heck, especially when it came time for revision. I longed for a computer but knew there was no way in the world I was going to be able to afford one anytime soon.

That Christmas, my parents apologized that I didn't have many presents. Times were tough and they had to cut back. It was fine, I was happy with what I had received. When we were finished opening gifts, my mom looked at my dad and said, "Do you want to do it?" He got up and left the room. My sister pulled out a camera. I had no idea what was going on. My dad came back into the room with a large box and set it on my lap. Still confused, I tore open the paper, saw the word *laptop*, and immediately burst into tears. To this day it is the greatest gift I've ever received because of how much it cost my parents and how utterly surprised I was. Had I expected to get that laptop, opening it would have been fun, but it wouldn't have had as profound an impact on me as it did. It was the "hiddenness" of the gift that made it so wonderful.

Some of what makes God's hiddenness frustrating for Christians is the fact that we are so steeped in the opposite. In the Christian world, nothing is elusive. The entire Sunday churchgoing experience is centered around a man or woman walking onto the stage and teaching you, *very clearly*, about God. Our movies and stories are packaged in a way that does the thinking for the audience. This team won the game because they prayed. That girl's life got better because she accepted Jesus Christ as her Lord and Savior. We don't have to work for much anymore, because everything is designed to be fully understood, fully fleshed out, and there shall be no room for interpretation, because interpretation can lead to bad doctrine, heresy, blah, blah, blah.

I find it fascinating that Jesus didn't seem to care that hardly anyone understood His parables. Shoot, half the time people didn't understand Him when He spoke plainly! When Nicodemus sneaks over to Jesus' place in the night to avoid the scandal of meeting with Him, he is completely perplexed by Jesus' instruction that he has to be "born again." When Jesus tells the Pharisees that if they destroy the temple, He will raise it back up again in three days, no one understands what He is saying. And Jesus apparently didn't care a lick.

While God's hiddenness can be frustrating, it's His silence that most of us find truly problematic. For me as a father, I can't imagine not responding to my children when they call out to me, even if I want them to learn something. But my interactions with my children are on a completely physical plane, whereas God is dealing with the spirit. I'm also not trying to teach my children to have faith in me, whereas God is constantly trying to move us to a place of greater faith.

DUDE, JUST SHUT UP

The story of Joseph has been one of my favorites since I was young. It has a little bit of everything you need in a good yarn: jealousy, attempted murder, false accusations, and radical forgiveness. But it's easy to forget that this story covers many, many years of a man's life. And throughout most of it, God is utterly silent.

Our story begins with seventeen-year-old Joseph, who apparently doesn't have the greatest level of social awareness. He is his father, Jacob's, favorite kid, and Jacob doesn't even try to hide that fact from his other kids. I guess Jacob wasn't reading up on the latest parenting books of the day, because this is numero uno for parenting no-nos. Scripture makes it plain—Joseph's brothers couldn't stand him.

When I was a kid, something happened that had a profound effect on me. I attended the same Lutheran school for eight years, and it was a small enough school that for the most part I had the same classmates every year. In all school situations, especially back then, you had a kind of hierarchy of "cool." This had almost nothing to do with who you were as a person but consisted mostly of athletic ability and not acting like a weirdo. No matter the sport, I was always picked third, which was more than respectable. I was invited to all the birthday parties, and I spent every weekend hanging out with my friends from school. Life was great, and I was happy.

Then one day everything changed. I still have no idea why or how it happened, but I remember going to school and suddenly everyone was making fun of me. And I mean everyone. It wasn't just my close friends giving me a good ribbing, this was every boy in my class, and it didn't let up. Even my teachers started ribbing me. I could have handled a day or two, but when weeks went by, I knew something was seriously wrong. I started getting picked dead last for sports, with people even groaning that they were stuck with me. I stopped getting invited to birthday parties, and the few that I did go to, no one wanted to do much with me. At lunch, my friends wouldn't let me sit with them anymore, and they banished me to the "dork table." So I ate lunch by myself. I remember coming home every day in tears, and my mom would just sit and hold me while I cried. I didn't understand what had happened. It was as if my entire class got together one day and decided to make me a pariah.

Luckily that was my final year at the school. After that it was off to high school, and I'd mercifully be able to start over someplace new with peers who didn't know anything about me. By the end of that eighth-grade year, I had pretty much lost all my friends. Instead of being sad to leave, I couldn't wait to get out of there.

All that to say, I know what it's like to have people "hate" you and not speak a kind word to you. I also learned early on in my personal hell that it was always best to just keep your mouth shut. If you talk, you draw attention to yourself and open yourself up to more insults. So when Joseph tattles on his brothers for mis-behaving while tending the flocks (Gen. 37:2), he had to know the heat he was putting on himself. And when he has a series of dreams that are clearly about his brothers being subservient to him (Gen. 37:5–7, 9), for the life of me I can't figure out why he told them. Maybe Joseph was still developing his emotional intelligence. But a smart person would write the dream down or maybe just tell it to his father.

Of course that's just the human side of the story. The real point of these dreams was for God to speak His promise over Joseph's life to him. He showed Joseph what his ultimate destiny would be at the age of seventeen, and I wonder how often Joseph thought about those dreams and what they could mean. What matters most is that God spoke to Joseph about His intention over his life.

Later on, Joseph's brothers have taken the herd far afield in an effort to find greener pastures, and Jacob sends Joseph to check on them and see how everything is going. Joseph sets out, stops at one point to ask for directions, then approaches his brothers. When they see him coming, they begin to plot his murder (geez, I guess they really *did* hate him), but thankfully Reuben, the oldest brother, keeps his head and talks them down to simply throwing Joseph down a well. Secretly he plans on coming back later and pulling him out. He probably hopes it will jar Joseph awake to tread more carefully with what he says to the bros.

They grab Joseph, tear off his precious robe, and throw him down the cistern. They then show their stone-cold hearts by sitting down and eating lunch while Joseph screams and pleads for his life. At some point, Reuben takes off, probably to check on some sheep. While he's gone, a caravan of merchants passes by and the brothers decide to sell Joseph into slavery instead of killing him (how merciful). When Reuben returns, he finds out Joseph is gone, and the brothers concoct a story to cover their tracks.

Things move quickly for us, the reader, but definitely not for Joseph. After he arrives in Egypt, he gets sold again to one of Pharaoh's officials, a guy named Potiphar. This is the best possible outcome for Joseph, but you can only imagine the fear and terror that a seventeen-year-old kid is feeling as his entire life of freedom and happiness has been ripped out from under him by his own family.

Thankfully, Joseph soon catches the eye of Potiphar and the powerful man clearly sees that Joseph has some real favor on his life. Everything he does seems to prosper. So Potiphar puts Joseph in charge of his entire estate, and Joseph responds by absolutely crushing it. Since God's favor is on Joseph, it's now on Potiphar as well, and he's so happy with Joseph's golden touch that he basically gives Joseph his job. All he has to worry about is whether he's going to have the chicken parm or the prime rib for dinner tonight.

From the moment Joseph received the dreams from God up to this point, he has, for the most part, lived a charmed life. Sure there was that little "sold into slavery" hiccup where for a few weeks he was in pure survival mode, but once he finally landed somewhere, the favor over his life returned. God was with him.

We often find ourselves in a similar place. When things are going well, doors are opening for us, finances are good, everyone is healthy and happy, and we have promises from God along with God's favor, which obviously means He's super happy with us right now. We're solid. We have no idea what was going through Joseph's mind during this time, but my guess is that as everything continues to work out in his favor, he continues to remember those dreams the Lord gave him and knows he's on the path to a wonderful destiny.

And then the hoochie mama shows up.

At this point, Joseph is a full-grown man, and not only does he have the favor of God on his life, he's also got male model looks (actually, I'm kind of starting to hate this guy too). Potiphar's wife has been eyeballing Joseph for a while, and one day she puts on her sexiest dress and attempts to seduce him. Joseph, though, is a man of highest integrity, and he refuses. He also seems to have learned his lesson on tattling, although this might have been one of those moments when it would have been wise to tell his boss what his wife was up to. But he doesn't, and the attempted seduction continues day after day. Finally, she corners him and tries to force him into bed. He has no other choice but to bolt, leaving his cloak still in her hand.

Apparently Joseph has a knack for finding the people around him with black hearts, because hell hath no fury like this woman scorned. She is in such a rage that she concocts a fake rape story and poisons Potiphar's mind against Joseph. And just like that, Joseph is thrown into prison.

What was Joseph thinking at this point? The narrative tells us that God continued to be with him in prison, and he winds up being put in charge of everything there as well. But come on, it's prison. He's a slave in prison. I wonder at what point he begins to question God's promises, the dreams God gave him. If he's anything like the rest of us, there must have been nights filled with some serious soul searching.

A while later, Joseph interprets the dreams of two inmates who had worked for Pharaoh, the cupbearer and the baker. He nails both interpretations, and pleads with them to remember him when they get out, to work some channels on his behalf because he's innocent. And of course, as soon as they're out, they completely forget about Joseph. Well, the baker is killed by Pharaoh, so I guess he's off the hook.

And now we reach the point of why I brought up this story.

"When two full years had passed, Pharaoh had a dream" (Gen. 41:1 NIV). Two years! That's 730 days. 17,520 hours. More than 1 million minutes. For us, it's one sentence. For Joseph, it must have been the pit of despair. The best years of his life are being wasted in prison for a crime he didn't commit, and there doesn't appear to be any end in sight. God has gone silent. His favor has lifted. When does the harsh reality wash over him like ice water? His brothers and father were right, he's just a dreamer. God isn't with him anymore. God is gone.

When the silent seasons come upon us, it almost always feels like abandonment. We wonder what we did wrong. We try to do better, pray more, give more—anything to shake God's voice awake again. If God was speaking at one time but isn't anymore, our natural thought is to believe that it is somehow our fault. That God is angry at us, or punishing us—putting us in time-out for our transgressions.

Joseph did nothing wrong, yet God allowed him to languish in an Egyptian prison for more than two years. The frustrated among us would look at his story and ask God, why couldn't You have given Pharaoh the dream a week after the cupbearer was restored to his post? Why not get Joseph out of prison sooner, give him more of his life back?

We've already discussed that we will never be able to fully understand all the ins, outs, whats, and whys of the things that happen in our lives, nor can we see the spiritual battles raging around us that bring both the good and the bad in our personal narratives, but we can be certain of one thing in either circumstance. God says, "They will be my people, and I will be their God. . . . I will never stop doing good to them . . . I will rejoice in doing them good . . . with all my heart and soul" (Jer. 32:38, 40–41 NIV).

God's great desire is to bless you. His promise is to never stop doing good to you. It brings Him great joy to do good for you. It is His heart and soul to do good things for you.

Even as tragedies piled up for Joseph, God was clear that He never left him. God didn't want Joseph's brothers to sell him into slavery, but He turned it to good for Joseph. God didn't want Joseph to be thrown into prison on false charges, but He turned it to good for Joseph.

Okay, you say, that's great. But why so long? Why the long

wait and extended silence? In fact, why does God go silent with us at all?

Throughout our lives, we learn to grab hold of God and communicate with Him in certain ways. We hold on to a certain aspect of Him that brings us comfort or joy, and to us that time and experience with Him is the most precious thing in the world. It's the glue that holds our faith together, the seat upon which our love affair with Jesus rests. When we talk of "relationship" with God, this particular interaction or view of Him is usually what we mean.

But that's not all of God. It's not even close. It's simply all we currently know and experience of Him.

What if God goes silent to encourage us to find a new aspect of Him, of His character, and a new way to interact with Him? When the old way of doing things no longer works, as long as we stick with Him, eventually we will find Him again. But this time we will know Him better, and our faith will have evolved into something more substantial. Maybe He goes silent in one way so we will learn to hear Him in another way.

Where we get into trouble is by taking any of this personally. Everything God does is soaked in love, and therefore if He does go silent for a season, it is out of love for us. He wants us to continue to grow, because He is also aware of what we're going to need for that next season when we are sold into slavery by our brothers, or are thrown into jail on false charges, or are given authority over the most powerful nation in the world.

Maybe you hear God through worship. But then one day, your ability to hear Him through worship dries up. Is God angry at you? Has He abandoned you? Of course not. But you need Him like you need air. So what do you do? Maybe you turn back to the

Scriptures, jump deeper into a Bible that you haven't paid much attention to during all your soaking sessions. Maybe you begin to find new aspects of God in the psalms. Maybe you learn what it means to hold fast to God's Word more than a prophetic word. Maybe . . . maybe . . . maybe . . .

We get frustrated because we think God is silent, but maybe He's simply hit the mute button because He wants you to change the channel and discover something new about Him, something new about yourself, something new about faith and love and devotion. The trouble comes when we never change the channel. Our faith gets broken when we hold so tightly to the ways we've always heard Him and then grow so frustrated and fearful that He's abandoned us because of the silence that we simply walk away from Him. Or we become fine with not hearing anything anymore. And we accept a stunted relationship, figuring this must be God's will for us. And we wonder what's wrong with us. And we wonder what's wrong with God.

The question is never with God's voice. It is always with our ability to hear and adapt to what He might be saying and how He might be saying it.

The reality is, God is always talking to us. Even in His silence He speaks.

/12/

THE ONLY TRUTH YOU
NEED TO KNOW

If there is one thing I have learned while on this epic journey of discovery in making films and going after the "more" of God, it's that we humans have a horrible habit of making things, and especially God, more complicated than we need to. I *do* realize that God is *way* more vast and, yes, complicated, than we will ever comprehend, but I'm not talking about who He is in His fullness. Instead, I'm talking about how we view Him. Because the goal, remember, is to renew our minds, our thoughts, and our understanding of God's love.

We Christians seem to really enjoy telling other people what we believe about God, but almost always with the intention of getting others to believe the same way we do. Shoot, that's pretty much what this entire book is trying to do! But while I hope some of the lessons I've learned about God have helped you, I would be remiss to end this book without stating the essence of who God is.

"God is love" (1 John 4:8).

If the Bible were to be distilled down to one simple phrase, I think that would be it. Every story, every action, every teaching is designed to display the core characteristic of God. *Love.* Even though God's anger burns against sin, nowhere in the Bible is He described as anger or wrath. There are two primary "God is" statements in the entire Bible that are designed to describe God's nature. The first is love. The second: "God is light; in him there is no darkness at all" (1 John 1:5 NIV). I find this fascinating. We find many other sides of His character and personality, but only two overt descriptions of His very nature. Love and light.

Look at all the objections I used to have about God based on who I thought He was: Selfish. Unkind. Self-absorbed. Uncaring. A task master. Zero empathy. Cold and clinical. Distant. Always angry. None of these descriptions match someone who is pure love and pure light.

Because God is God, we tend to think that He has basically signed off on all our experiences. We won't blame Him, per se, but we will take offense that He didn't seem to do anything to stop the bad from happening. As a result, many of us have a kind of passive-aggressive faith.

While I will wholeheartedly state that whatever good happens in our lives *is* a result of God's goodness and blessing ("Every good and perfect gift is from above, coming down from the Father of the heavenly lights, who does not change like shifting shadows" James 1:17 NIV), I cannot say with certainty what troubles in my life are sent by Him and which ones are attacks from the enemy. I do know two incontrovertible facts: the Devil comes to steal, kill, and destroy my life, and God is always working for my good out of an everlasting love for me. If God is able to take something the Devil meant for evil and turn it around for good, then that is God's graciousness working for my life. We get into trouble, though, when we filter everything that happens as originating from the will and desire of God.

Ah yes, that pesky filter of ours. It's so fickle, so self-absorbed, and so very unreliable. There is a reason that God's Word must be our baseline anchor for our understanding of God, because unlike us, it never changes. We want answers to every question, and when those answers are slow in coming, we tend to create personal theologies to help us cope with the unknown.

I am a man with a lot of questions about God—shoot, I created an entire television series about it! But understanding more of God is like pulling on an infinite string—you're never going to get to the end. As soon as one question is answered, three more pop up. Which is why I am okay with not knowing the answer to everything and just resting in some simple truths about who God is.

ALL YOU NEED TO KNOW

God is love. And if God is indeed love personified, then all the attributes of love apply to Him. Let's look at some of these qualities as they are laid out for us in 1 Corinthians 13:4–8 and see what they really mean. (All definitions in this section are from Dictionary.com.)

He Is Patient

Patience: The bearing of provocation, annoyance, misfortune, or pain, without complaint, loss of temper, irritation, or the like. An ability or willingness to suppress restlessness or annoyance when confronted with delay. Quiet, steady perseverance; even-tempered care, diligence.

Think of how often we misrepresent God to others and how annoying that must be to Him. Think of how much pain we've inflicted on Him and others He loves through our poor choices, sinful behavior, and outright rebellion. God is not like us in how He reacts. He doesn't sneak off into the break room with the Holy Spirit and Jesus and spew out His frustrations with us. He doesn't lose His temper, doesn't wake up in a bad mood some days, doesn't get irritated with us. God has plans for our lives, plans for us to prosper, but most of the time we get in the way of those plans and delay them by our own issues, mistrust, and desire to do what we want to do. Literally every major blessing that has happened to me came simply because I was obedient to what the Lord was asking me to do. Every one.

I used to think God wanted me to be obedient to somehow prove I was a good company man. I used to think obedience was a perpetual test that I either passed or failed. It was all designed for Him to see if He could trust me. But that's not friendship—and it certainly isn't love.

The reality is that our obedience opens up the means by which God can work on our behalf. Our choices are only important in as much as they are done in obedience to what God is asking of us. His desire for obedience isn't a test, it's an opportunity. Unlike us, God knows the entire situation, all the nuances, every possible outcome based on a wide variety of choices, and when He is asking us to trust Him on something, rest assured that request has been infinitely thought out. If we could get over ourselves and stop thinking we need to retain control of our lives, we would begin to walk in blessings we never imagined.

Of course, His patience doesn't just extend to us, but to everyone. We love it when God has grace and patience for our own idiot choices, but as soon as He extends it to people who we think need a good kick in the pants, suddenly it feels like indulgence on God's part. We see the destruction their choices are causing, and we want God to step in and stop it. Meanwhile, we are completely ignoring the destruction *our* choices are causing. We are hopelessly stuck in the moment, but God isn't. His patience is always working on our behalf to bring about repentance, forgiveness, and obedience.

He Is Kind

Kind: of a good or benevolent nature or disposition.
Considerate, helpful, humane. Mild, gentle.

I know the first thing you're thinking right now. What does *benevolent* mean? Don't worry, I'm here to help. It means "desiring to help others; intended for benefits rather than profit." Thus ends our word of the day.

The kindness of God isn't talked about nearly as much as it should be. It is interesting to note that it is this kindness that sparks repentance: "Or do you presume on the riches of his kindness and forbearance and patience, not knowing that *God's kindness is meant to lead you to repentance*?" (Rom. 2:4).

We think that conviction is what is needed for repentance, which is certainly true, but I think we miss the mark quite often regarding the mechanism by which conviction is reached. We think fear—whether it's for our eternal souls or the fear of consequences—is the best delivery system for conviction, but according to God, that isn't the case. Fear is the *opposite* of love. It is God's kindness, His ultimate desire for our good, that brings us to our knees and breaks our hearts enough to want to turn from our sinful, rebellious choices.

God's natural state is one of benevolence (see, you know it now!). I was convinced that God was only interested in getting what He wanted from me, that He simply wanted to profit off of me. After all, leading others to Jesus profits the person getting saved and God—I'm just the mule He's asking to do the work for Him. So get in line, do what you're told, make yourself uncomfortable because it's probably good for you, but really it's all about God getting what He wants. I believed God simply wanted to *use* me, and not in the positive intention of that word.

But if God is love, and that love is kind, then God is more interested in our benefit than in His profit margins. It's the reason He will leave the ninety-nine sheep to find the lost one. For many people this is not only hard to believe but equally hard to accept. I think it's because we are so used to people of power using that power for themselves, but with God it is the opposite. He takes the form of a servant. When Jesus wants to make perfectly clear how the kingdom of God is supposed to roll, He gets down on His knees and washes feet. He's the Master, but He washes our feet, binds up our wounds, and wipes away our tears.

Even when He's disciplining David after his big failure, God shows this nature when He tells David, "I gave you everything you desired, and if it wasn't enough for you I would have given you even more!" We are not dealing with a despot or a cruel taskmaster here. We're dealing with someone whose very nature is to give and pour out blessings.

He is mild. God isn't a spicy meatball. It's hard to reconcile the mildness of God when we have pictures of Him literally blowing up a mountain when He descends upon it in Exodus 19, or when someone is struck dead for simply grabbing hold of the ark of the covenant to keep it from sliding off a cart. But then we see Jesus, the perfect representation of the Father, standing in front of a woman caught in the act of adultery, and all that He does is tender and kind.

He's gentle with us. There is a reason sinners flocked to Jesus. There is a reason the "bad" people of society would hang with Him at a party all night. Jesus didn't always pull out a whip of judgment but rather brought a gentle peace to every person drowning in sickness, brokenness, and sin. Christians have too often represented God as being angry at people, especially people struggling with sin. But Jesus described Himself as a doctor who came to bring life to the sick and dying. A doctor walks headlong into a disease-ridden room, he doesn't require that the people clean themselves up before he will see them.

He Does Not Envy

Envy: a feeling of discontent or covetousness with regard to another's advantages, success, possessions, etc.

This one doesn't seem too hard to grasp. God is God, after all. Why would He ever envy anything when He already *has* everything? God doesn't need anything from us. He doesn't need our skill sets, our personalities, our way with words, our talents, or our intelligence. He doesn't need our strengths, our resources, our wealth. He doesn't look at whatever it is you do well and desire it for Himself or even His purposes. He will use it if you offer it up to Him, for sure, but an offering is a lot different from a hostile takeover.

He Does Not Boast

Boast: to speak with excessive pride or vanity.

Not only does God not have an ounce of pride in Him, but pride is something He actively hates and combats. James 4:6 tells us that "God *opposes the proud* but gives grace to the humble." When we operate out of pride and arrogance, God raises His hand in opposition. Humble people realize who they truly are in the grand scheme of things, and they are, quite frankly, people you love to be around. When God talks of His "great and mighty power," it is a simple fact. The fact that He's the one saying it doesn't matter. Because it's true.

He Is Not Arrogant

Arrogance: offensive display of superiority or self-importance; overbearing pride.

Even though God has every right to display His superiority and importance over us, He instead chooses to do the opposite. He washes feet. He encourages the little children to come to Him even though the disciples are trying to pull the VIP card. He allows His body to be broken and destroyed to pay for our screwups.

Some might say that God's constant "thou shalt have no other gods before me" talk is a form of superiority, but that's a miscalculation of God's heart. God's great desire is to have a relationship with us, to return the world to the way it was in the garden. When we bring other gods into our lives, He doesn't get upset because He's prideful, He gets upset because our relationship suffers. Allowing other things to become gods in your life is the equivalent of cheating on God. He's a jealous God for sure, but His jealousy is not rooted in some brokenhearted, fearful, control-based mania, but rather in a burning desire for purity in our relationship with Him. His love never fades from us, nor does He ever ignore or waver from us. We're the ones who constantly walk away from Him. And His reaction is always the same—pursuit.

He Is Not Rude

Rude: discourteous or impolite; without refinement; rough, harsh, or ungentle.

Being a minor public figure whose work tends to elicit pretty strong reactions, I have seen both the best and the worst that people have to offer. And unfortunately, I have found that in most of my dealing with people, Christians by far can be the rudest people on the planet. When Christianity is no longer a relationship with a loving God, it can quickly devolve into dogmatic theological bullying. One cursory look at social media could make you never want to hang out with Christians again! The judgments, the lecturing, the name-calling, the gossiping, even the foul language used when faced with something spiritual that someone doesn't agree with are astounding.

People like this use Jesus as their example, but in a way that completely twists what He did into something grotesque. For instance, Jesus was constantly harping at the religious leaders of His day, and often they told Him they thought He was being rude. And He'd just lay into them even more. Sometimes Christians think this gives them a license to lay into fellow Christians they think are in error. But Jesus was not upset that the religious people were in error theologically, He was upset because they made experiencing God so much more difficult than it needed to be! The Pharisees were physically keeping people from God's true nature, which is like keeping my kids from me. If you try to make it impossible for my kids to be with me, I'm going to have some very strong words for you. And Jesus was no different.

But these armchair theologians and internet trolls are not upset by this at all. Often they're upset because people are making it *too* easy to find God! They want people to really "feel" their own sinfulness, not understanding that people feel their sin every day, even if they don't yet understand what the feeling is. Talk to anyone who comes out of a life of sin into God's grace and forgiveness and they'll tell you they always knew something was deeply wrong. They just didn't know what could be done about it. So they tried to mask the pain of their reality with substances or sex or video games or shopping or eating or whatever. But after the Holy Spirit shows up in their lives, the whole scene shifts— everything changes on the inside.

There are certain theological positions today that drive me up a wall (the prosperity gospel and hyper-grace at the top of the list), but I never want to get to a place where, in my desire to overcome these theological traps, I become rude and belligerent. We have been called to love even our enemies, but the way many Christians act online, you'd think there are some people who are worse than enemies, so our love doesn't have to extend to them.

He Does Not Insist on His Own Way

This one doesn't need a dictionary definition, but I think it might be one of the most explosive revelations of God's love in the whole list. I was always taught that God is in total control and that He's simply moving all the chess pieces around as He wills in order to get His own way. But now He's telling us that love does not insist on its own way. So what gives?

Well obviously, what I was taught is wrong. Free will is proof of the purity of God's love. He offers us total freedom to choose Him or not, do right or not, act in love or not. God definitely *works* toward the outcomes He desires, but He never forces anyone to do anything, nor does He stop you from thwarting His plans. When our free will causes a break in His perfect plan, God simply reroutes and comes at His will from another angle, like a heavenly GPS. I think that's why Jesus even tells us to pray for God's will to be done here on earth as it is in heaven. God's perfect will is complete in heaven, but down here He has to deal with six billion morons who would rather operate according to their own will than His.

God is always working for your good (yes, even when bad things happen to you), but the only way to receive the fullness of His will over your life, to receive the good He intends for you, is for you to place all your trust in Him and what He is asking you to do today.

He Is Not Irritable

Irritated: angered, provoked, or annoyed.

Irritation is such a basic human emotion, I think it's hard for us to believe that God isn't constantly irritated by how much we screw up on a regular basis. The afterhaze of sin sinks us into that state of mind where we are certain that God has finally had enough of our sinful behavior and He's about to blow a gasket. And as hard as I tried, I couldn't ignore those stories in the Bible where it sure seemed like He *did* blow a gasket.

In Deuteronomy 9, God appears to have finally gotten to a point with the Jewish people that we all feel He's about to get to with us: "The LORD spoke further to me [Moses], saying, 'I have seen this people, and indeed, it is a stubborn people. Let Me alone, that I may destroy them and blot out their name from under heaven; and I will make of you a nation mightier and greater than they'" (Deut. 9:13–14 NASB).

That's what my flesh tries to tell me God is going to do whenever I screw up for the one thousandth time. It's what causes us to run and hide from Him, because no one wants to get beaten by a holy belt. God is obviously angry with His people here, and you see it time and time again throughout Scripture where God states His displeasure at the constant rejection and sinning of His people. So God definitely gets angry at our sin. But anger is different from irritation. God is never annoyed by us, and He can somehow put up with even the most challenging personalities.

It is also important to note that most of God's anger happens before the cross comes into the picture. Jesus' sacrifice has assured us of an eternity of forgiveness, grace, and love at the hands of God. Our debt has been paid, even as we pile on more and more debt through bad decisions. Consequences will still come calling for our sinful choices, but punishment never will.

He Is Not Resentful

Resent: to feel or show displeasure or indignation from a sense of injury or insult.

I have been wronged on some deep, personal levels over the years, and I've worked hard to walk in radical forgiveness for those who've hurt me, but it's still hard to let go of some of those things. Someone says or does something, and that triggers the past pain you thought you'd already dealt with. As much as we want to leave our trauma and the sins of others against us in the past when we choose forgiveness, memory is a fickle thing, and it doesn't always cooperate with our hearts.

I think one of the most dangerous things we can do is anthropomorphize God—that is, turn our understanding of Him into that of a human being. But God is not a man, and His ways are higher than our ways. So when He says something like this, He means it: "He has removed our sins as far from us as the east is from the west" (Ps. 103:12 NLT). And: "For I will forgive their wickedness and will remember their sins no more" (Heb. 8:12 NIV).

I don't know how God does it, but somehow, when He forgives us, He lets it go completely. Maybe that's the mark of ultimate forgiveness—that it never, ever comes up again, never twinges or triggers, is never a "thing" again. While we wallow in the afterhaze of sin and hide from Him in shame and guilt, He comes right for us, because we are His delight and His forgiveness is complete.

How can anyone not want a God as loving as this?

He Does Not Rejoice in Wrongdoing, but Rejoices with the Truth

There is one aspect to this explanation of love that I find fascinating. God actually "rejoices." I always had a view of the Father as a serious, austere, wooden personality. Even the stories of Jesus in the Gospels pretty much stick to the solid colors and hardly deal at all with the lighter side of the Almighty. But love rejoices with the truth, and what an amazing thought to think that God's Spirit rejoices over us when we walk in obedience and righteousness and truth.

He Bears All Things

Bear: to hold up, support; to hold firm under a load.

The human race has a capacity for selfishness, greed, wickedness, and evil that is breathtaking. Even the best of us have darkness in our hearts that, when recognized, surprises us with its ferocity of evil intent. But God is love, and as such He is somehow able to bear our destructive and devastating decisions. He sticks with us, continues to pursue us, holds firm to His hope for us. His love never wanes, it never gets tired or worn out. He can hold up under the strain of our lifetime of screwups, temper tantrums, betrayals, abandonment, and prideful insistence on our own way. God bears it all. When I look at the level of evil in the world, this might be one of His most impressive attributes of all.

He Believes All Things

Believe: to have a conviction that (a person or thing) is, has been, or will be engaged in a given action or involved in a given situation; to have confidence in the assertions of (a person).

God believes in you. For many this will be hard to accept, but it's true. He believes in your best qualities. He believes you will make the right decision next time. He believes in your abilities. He believes in all good things surrounding your life, your personality, your level of faith, and your actions.

God believed that I could make films that changed the world in some small way, even though at the time He called me I was far from Him, wanted nothing to do with Him or the Holy Spirit, and wasn't even interested in making movies. But as usual, He knew better. He saw something inside of me—maybe it was my devout stance that I only want what is 100 percent real, and all this God stuff I was encountering felt mostly like fluff and good intentions and an attempt to keep churches and pastors in business. Maybe He understood then that He could trust me with some of His most precious stories, because deep down I am just a hobbit and I don't want to be famous and I don't want to go on radical adventures.

Whatever it was, God saw something He liked, and He believed that I was the man He saw, even when I had given Him absolutely no reason to think such things. But He reached out for me anyway, I think, in large part because . . .

He Hopes All Things

Hope: the feeling that what is wanted can be had or that events will turn out for the best.

God believes you are who He says you are, and His hope that you will get to where He is calling you never stops. I used to think God's natural state was to be against me, but the opposite is true. When He turns His eyes on you, His natural inclination isn't to feel anger or disappointment or annoyance—He feels none of those things for you. His first thought for you is one of hope. Because He knows you're not a loser. He knows you actually do want to live a life of purity and righteousness. He knows you really do want to put all of your trust in Him and walk in radical obedience to Him. He knows that you really do love Him. He knows all these things about you, and He continues to hope that one day you will see them too. And why does He hope? Because He knows that He will never stop working for your good and for your heart, and as long as He's still on the job, there will always be hope.

He Endures All Things

Endure: to bear without resistance or with patience; to allow; to last.

The word *tolerance* means different things for different people. To some Christians it's become a dirty word that implies a weak view on sin. To others it is a lifeboat to cling to in order to avoid the judgment of others for their choices. To still others it is a rallying cry. To some it is a political hammer they use to hack down their opposition, but never to be applied in their own worldview toward their opposition. In my opinion, we've pretty much lost this word to any one meaning. It has been so fractured and desecrated, placed atop so many political, sexual, and moral hills, that it can no longer be viewed as one, objective thing. It's the perfect postmodern word for a postmodern world.

But when God says that He endures all things, He is being quite clear, and it may not go over well with many Christians. Because what God is talking about here is, dare I say it, tolerance. But it is a certain kind of tolerance, one that is fully objective and rooted to the spot. God's tolerance isn't going anywhere, and it will not be subject to the winds of politics or the whims of society.

God's tolerance, His endurance, "bears without resistance." It is patient. Some Christians get frustrated because we now live in a culture where if you disagree with the mob mentality of morality, then you are labeled intolerant. But disagreement with something is not intolerance. God disagrees with our sin constantly, and He is the most tolerant being in the universe. But I think there might be something we Christians are missing when it comes to engaging with our culture. I have yet to meet any two people who have the exact same views on everything in life. No one fully agrees with even one other person in the world, let alone millions. But it is what you do with that disagreement that defines whether or not you are intolerant.

When Jesus told us to turn the other cheek when someone hits us, I don't think He was only talking about physical assault. Being assaulted for what you believe is not a fun experience. I get it all the time from internet trolls, and it never feels good. In fact, it always feels like a slap in the face, a shot at my faith and character. And I can either choose to engage and fight back, or I can simply walk away, forgive them, and not engage in a morality fistfight.

I've had my seasons of raging at God, of believing the worst of Him, of not wanting anything to do with Him because of who I thought He was. Shoot, I've laid most of them out for you here in this book. But not once in my life did God ever fire back at me. Never did He send a prophet to bring me low, to ring me upside the head and tell me how dumb and terrible I was for believing all these lies about Him. No, God tolerated and endured my immaturity, my moral bankruptcy, and my bad theology. He loved me, blessed me, continued to "work all things for my good" even though I was a grade-A jerk.

I'm all for trying to turn the tide of morality in our culture, but I don't think we're ever going to get there by trying to scream louder than everyone else. I don't think we can buy our way there, nor can we use politics to bring truth to the world. As trite as it might sound these days, the world just needs Jesus. They need a God who can be so calm in a storm that He falls asleep, and when He wakes up merely needs to speak a word and the storm will cease.

But for whatever reason, God has chosen us—His little Christs—to bear His name to the world. And obviously we're doing a poor job of it, but that doesn't faze God. He believes in His bride. He has hope that one day she will get it, that she will finally understand the kingdom, and she will become an agent of love to the world around her, even as that world spits in her face, takes shots at her, disparages her reputation, and lies and cheats on her. Because when that day comes, the bride will believe in her fellow man the way God believes in her, and the bride will hope that they, too, will one day meet the same Jesus who transformed her.

He Never Ends

The only true constant in the world is that God is love, and that His love will never end. God will never give up on you. He will never stop loving you. Even when you blame Him for your problems, believe false things about Him, curse at Him, crucify Him—He'll never stop loving you.

This is the only thing you need to know. As Jesus hung on the cross, completely naked, the flesh torn from His body, a crown of thorns on His head, and masses of people mocking Him and hating Him, He had one reaction.

Father, forgive them. They don't know what they're doing.

He said it then.

He still says it today.

You're chasing a God you don't want to catch, but it's time to stop running. It's time to stop chasing. The whole time you think you've been running for Him, you've actually been running from Him. Because He is the one who pursues. He is the one who wants you.

So stop chasing Him.

Turn around.

Let Him catch you.

ACKNOWLEDGMENTS

I want to thank my editor on this sucker, Janene MacIvor, for walking that fine line with me of writing something that is fun without being offensive. (I'm still taking a hard stance on that ONE word, Janene!) You were a great creative partner on this thing.

I also want to thank my pops, Gary Wilson, who always showed me that no question is out of bounds and that it's okay to wrestle with God sometimes.

To everyone else who made this book possible, to the whole team at HarperCollins and Emanate Books, you guys are awesome. Thank you for all your great work.

ABOUT THE AUTHOR

Darren Wilson is the founder of WP Films, a film/television production company that focuses on creating media that creatively and powerfully advances the kingdom of God around the world. He is also an author and a speaker. Darren's films have been seen by millions around the world and have helped change the spiritual climate of the worldwide church. In addition to his films and television work, Darren is the author of four books and speaks as often as his busy schedule allows. Devon Franklin, VP of Production for Columbia Pictures, called Darren "one of the most innovative filmmakers and authors of faith today." Find out more about Darren and his work at wpfilm.com.